Essential Law

Criminal Law & Procedure

Self-Teaching Guide

3rd edition

STERLING
Education

This publication is designed to provide accurate and authoritative information regarding the subject matter covered. It is distributed with the understanding that the publisher, authors, or editors are not engaged in rendering legal or another professional service. If legal advice or other expert assistance is required, competent professional services should be sought. Sterling Education is not legally liable for mistakes, omissions, or inaccuracies in this publication's content.

3   2   1

ISBN-13: 979-8-8855701-1-4

Sterling Education products are available at quantity discounts.

Contact info@sterling–prep.com.

Sterling Education
6 Liberty Square #11
Boston, MA 02109

Customer Satisfaction Guarantee

Your feedback is important because we strive to provide the highest quality prep materials. Email us comments or suggestions.

info@sterling–prep.com

We reply to emails – check your spam folder

STERLING
Education

From the foundations of constitutional law to complex issues of contracts, the *Essential Law Self-Teaching Guide* series is a perfect compendium to help readers understand multifaceted areas of American Law. Created by highly qualified legal professionals with extensive credentials, these books empower readers to expand their understanding of law.

The content is a clearly presented and systematically organized review of legal principles governing various areas of law. It elucidates the concepts of constitutional rights, criminal law, civil procedure, rules of evidence, contracts, torts, real property, family law, estates, wills and trusts, and business associations.

We commend your desire to learn more about the law. The editors sincerely hope that these guides will be a valuable resource for your learning.

Comprehensive Glossary of Legal Terms

Over 2,100 essential legal terms defined and explained. An excellent reference source for law students, practitioners, and readers seeking an understanding of legal vocabulary and its application.

Landmark U.S. Supreme Court Cases: Essential Summaries

Learn important constitutional cases that shaped American law. Understand how the evolving needs of society intersect with the U.S. Constitution. Summaries of seminal Supreme Court cases focused on legal issues, underlying principles, and judicial decisions.

Visit our Amazon store

Table of Contents

GOVERNING LAW (*continued*)

GOVERNING LAW (*continued*)

ANATOMY OF A LAWSUIT (*continued*)

APPENDIX (*continued*)

APPENDIX (*continued*)

APPENDIX (*continued*)

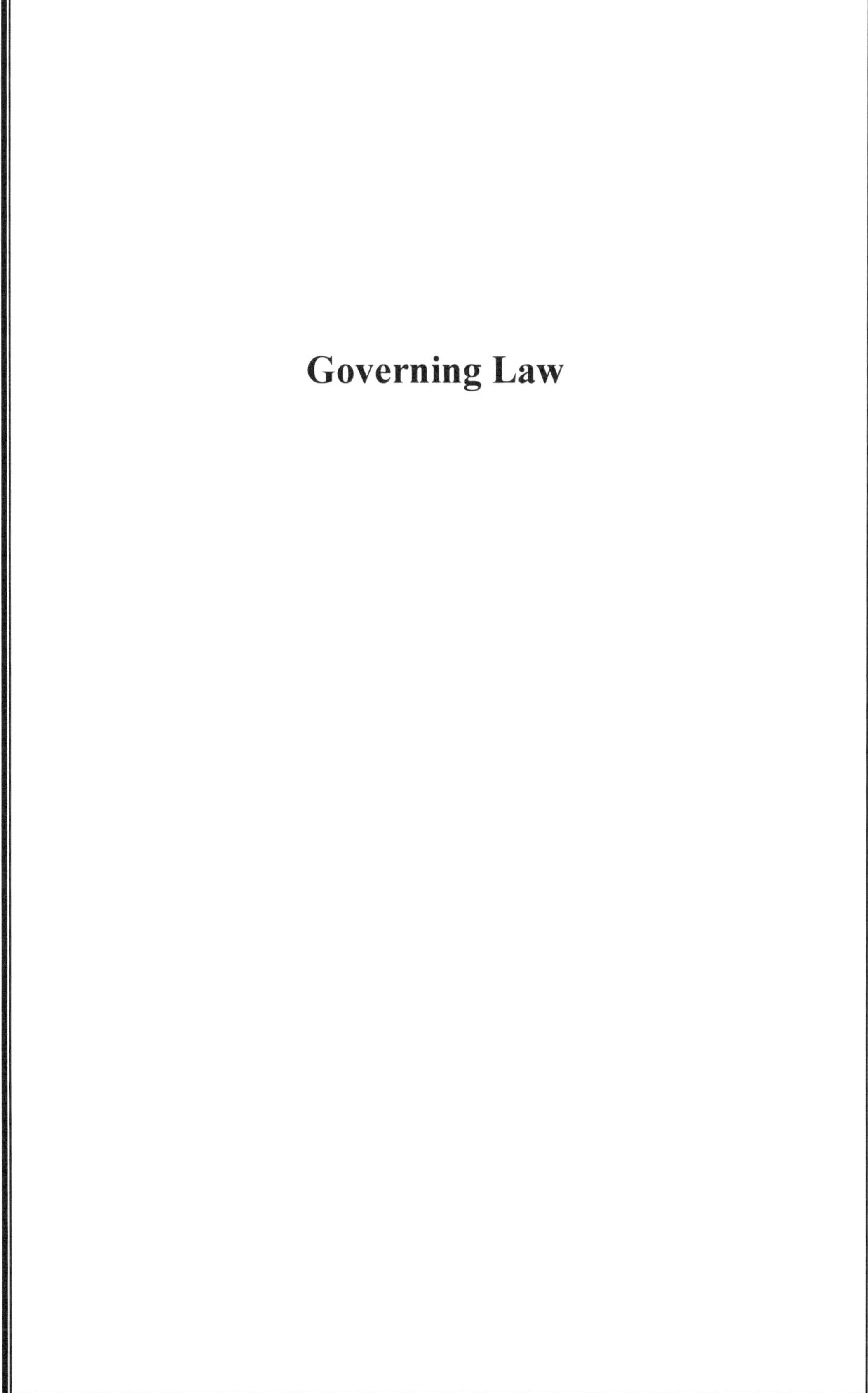

Governing Law

Homicide Crimes

For criminal homicide, the prosecution must show that the defendant's act was the proximate cause of the victim's death.

Murder

When the test uses a word like "murder" or "robbery" and provides no further definition of the crime, it refers to the common law crime.

Know the elements of common law crimes and apply them to specific facts.

If the question wants a definition of a crime different from the common law, they will either define the crime in the question or use a term such as "under modern law."

Definition of malice for common law murder

The mental state required for common law murder is malice.

Murder has four separate definitions.

1) Intent to kill.

2) Intent to do great bodily harm.

3) A death occurring in the course of a felony.

4) Willful and wanton disregard of an unreasonable risk (i.e., depraved heart killing).

A person under a duty to aid another because of a contractual or familial relationship is guilty of involuntary manslaughter if death occurs because of unreasonable failure to give that aid.

An intent to kill constitutes malice (*mens rea* for common law murder).

A defendant must have a mental state of *malice* when acting to end the victim's life to be guilty of murder.

Murder – intentional killings

Intent to kill has two definitions:

1) the desire to accomplish a specific result.

2) engaging in such actions that the result is inevitable even though not explicitly desired.

The motive behind that intent is irrelevant in establishing intent.

The killing of a terminally ill patient who pleads with a person to end their life is murder at common law because it is an intentional killing.

The consent of the victim is not a defense to intentional killing.

The doctrine of transferred intent makes the killing of an unintended victim an intentional killing if it occurs due to an intent to kill the victim.

If a person employs a mechanical device that kills a person when activated, the intent to set up the device is equivalent to the intent to activate it.

If there are no mitigating circumstances or defenses to the killing, the person setting up the device is guilty of murder.

An intentional killing by a person threatened with death if they do not complete the killing is murder; there is no defense of duress to murder.

Murder – intent to do great bodily harm

Inflicting severe bodily harm on a victim that was not likely to cause death constitutes murder if the victim dies due to the infliction of that serious bodily harm.

A single blow administered by a fist would not ordinarily give rise to an inference that the actor intended severe bodily harm; a severe and prolonged beating or kicking a victim indicates such intent.

The infliction of a wound with a gun or a knife or other weapon would ordinarily give rise to the inference that intent to do great bodily harm was present.

The victim must die from injuries inflicted with the intent to do serious bodily harm before this malice becomes the malice needed for murder.

Felony murder

Felony murder occurs only when the defendant is committing or attempting to commit a felony, which qualifies as a felony supporting felony murder.

If the defendant is not guilty of the underlying felony, they are not guilty of felony murder. Often this is the best defense to the charge of felony murder.

A person is not guilty of felony murder if the underlying felony has not commenced or is not completed when the death occurs.

Mayhem, **R**ape, **B**urglary, **A**rson, **K**idnapping, **E**scape and **R**obbery (acronym MR. BAKER) are common law felonies that support felony murder.

Manslaughter and assault and battery, even though common law felonies, cannot be the underlying felony for felony murder.

Neither intent to kill, nor intent to commit serious bodily harm, is an element of the malice necessary to support felony murder.

An intentional killing during a felony provides two bases of malice for common law murder.

A death that occurs during a conspiracy to commit a MR. BAKER felony constitutes felony murder, imputed to all conspirators when the killing occurs unless the killing was beyond the scope of the conspiracy (e.g., rape by one actor during a bank robbery).

The killing of a co-felon in the course of a felony by a third person does not sustain a felony murder charge against the surviving felon because, under the Redline rule, the killing is justifiable homicide.

Depraved heart murder

A defendant is guilty of murder if they engage in conduct involving a wanton and willful disregard of unreasonable human risk, resulting in death.

The reckless conduct must involve a substantial degree of risk to human life.

The risk involved is to be assessed considering what the defendant knows, and the risk taken must be unjustifiable under the circumstances.

Examples of conduct that constitute the malice for malignant heart murder (depraved heart murder) if death occurs because of the action are:

- firing bullets in a confined space, through a wall, or into an urban area for confusing police;

- playing Russian roulette;

- deliberately and unjustifiably driving a car onto a crowded sidewalk;

- using deceit to convince an individual to take action likely to get them killed.

Homicide exam questions

The wording of a question may require discarding the standard pecking order of analysis of homicide crimes.

Typically, felony murder is considered first-degree murder and more serious than murder under the depraved-heart doctrine.

A question may suggest that murder under the depraved-heart doctrine is more serious than killing during a common law felony in a specific situation.

It is crucial to carefully read the question and be prepared to suspend the standard principles of black letter law if the question reads that way.

Degrees of murder

Since there are no degrees of murder at common law, a question concerning degrees of murder will set forth a statute that controls how degrees of murder are calculated.

Many statutes define first-degree murder as killing with deliberate, premeditated malice aforethought, limiting first-degree murder to planned, intentional killings.

When the malice for murder intends to do great bodily harm or with the recklessness which constitutes depraved heart murder, the murder is usually classified as second-degree murder.

Voluntary manslaughter

To reduce a murder crime where the malice was either the intent to kill or intent to do great bodily harm, to voluntary manslaughter, there must be:

(a) adequate provocation to inflame a reasonable person into the heat of passion, and

(b) the defendant must have been in such a state, and

(c) the killing must have taken place at a time when the passions of a reasonable person would not have cooled, and those of the defendant did not cool.

Where the malice for murder is felony murder or depraved heart murder, there is no reduction of the murder crime to manslaughter.

A violent battery, witnessing or learning about spousal infidelity, mutual affray, and an illegal arrest satisfy the adequate provocation element of voluntary manslaughter.

Mere words, no matter how insulting, are not adequate provocation for violence.

A second basis for reducing murder to voluntary manslaughter is when the defendant has the right to self-defense or defend another. However, such a defense will not result in an acquittal because it was not properly perfected.

For example, a defendant only had a right to use non-deadly force to defend themself but used deadly force, or a defendant failed to retreat where the retreat doctrine was applicable.

Under the doctrine of *transferred intent*, the killing will be reduced from murder to manslaughter if the defendant killed the victim mistakenly when trying to kill another whose death would have resulted in manslaughter rather than a murder conviction.

Involuntary manslaughter

Willful, wanton conduct is behavior slightly less egregious than the conduct which forms the basis of malice in depraved heart murder.

A death caused by willful, wanton, but not the defendant's intentional conduct, is involuntary manslaughter.

If death occurs while the defendant is engaged in a misdemeanor, which is morally wrong (a misdemeanor *malum in se*), he/she is guilty of involuntary manslaughter.

Generally, there is no affirmative duty to aid a person in peril and no criminal liability on the person in a position to give aid who fails to provide aid.

A person is under a duty to aid if they have a contractual obligation to do so, their actions (or inactions) put the victim in peril, or there is a parent-child or other family relationship between the defendant and the victim.

In such circumstances, if the failure to render aid results in death, the refusal to give aid can constitute willful, wanton conduct, causing the defendant to be guilty of involuntary manslaughter.

A defendant must act in a willful, wanton manner in performing the act, ending the victim's life to be guilty of involuntary manslaughter.

An unreasonable belief concerning the defendant's threat of harm is not justification for engaging in willful, wanton conduct.

Elements for murder statutes

Note the terms of the statute given in the question, which separates murder into degrees.

Intentional killings and felony murder are two elements of malice classified as first-degree murder.

Intention to do great bodily harm and depraved heart murder are two elements of malice classified as second-degree murder.

For an intentional killing, determine if the intent was formed due to deliberate premeditation and whether circumstances reduce the crime to voluntary manslaughter or provide a total defense to the murder crime such as self-defense.

Self-defense

Deadly force is likely to cause death, whether or not death occurs in a particular instance.

Non-deadly force is not likely to cause death, even though death occurred.

A defendant who uses deadly force can successfully raise *self-defense* to a homicide charge if they reasonably believe they are in danger of death or great bodily harm, even if not actually in such danger.

A defendant who uses deadly force can successfully raise a defense if they used that deadly force to apprehend a dangerous felon or to prevent a dangerous felony from being committed

The defense is successful for misdemeanor crimes if the force used is non-deadly.

If a jurisdiction requires a person to retreat before using deadly force in self-defense, a retreat is not required if the person believes that there is no reasonable method of retreat or if attacked in their home.

Even though they are in danger of death or serious bodily harm, a defendant does NOT have the right of self-defense if:

- they are in the commission of a felony,

- a police officer lawfully arrests,

- they were the original aggressor, except when the original aggressor attacks with non-deadly force and is met with deadly force or unless they:

  1) completely terminates their status as an aggressor, and

  2) make that known to the person attacked.

Defense of property does not justify deadly force.

If a person has a valid right of self-defense against A and kills B by mistake, they have a defense to a charge that they murdered B because that killing is justified under the doctrine of *transferred intent*.

Defense of others

A person using deadly force to defend another, in the belief that the person defended has the right to use deadly force in self-defense, has a valid defense in a criminal prosecution, even if the person defended does not have the right of self-defense because the person defended was the original aggressor.

A person has the right to use the same force, defending others as they do defend themself.

The right to use the same force is not limited to family members.

Other defenses to homicide crimes

Justifiable homicide is a killing permitted by law, such as the killing by the executioner in a death penalty case or the killing by soldiers on the battlefield.

Justifiable homicide is not criminal homicide.

Duress occurs when an individual commits an act against their will because of a fear of death or substantial bodily harm threatened by another human being.

Necessity relates to coercion by nonhuman elements, such as natural forces threatening an individual's life.

Neither duress nor necessity is a defense to a homicide crime.

In a felony murder case, duress or necessity can be a defense to the underlying felony, thereby eliminating an essential element of felony murder.

Notes for active learning

Assault and battery

A criminal battery is the unlawful application of force, either by direct contact or indirect physical contact, to a person or recognized extension.

The force may be direct physical touching or using a gun (or another weapon) applied either against the body of the victim or something closely associated with the victim.

Intent or conduct amounting to criminal negligence forms the *mens rea* for battery.

A person has the right to use non-deadly force in self-defense if attacked with non-deadly force.

A defendant using non-deadly instead of deadly force in self-defense against an aggressor does not have to retreat.

The retreat doctrine only applies in limited circumstances to the use of deadly force against the aggressor.

Whether actual or implied, consent is a defense to assault and battery.

Rape

Consent to intercourse would be a defense to rape even if the defendant committed fraud in inducing the victim to have intercourse.

If the defendant commits fraud in the *factum* instead of fraud in the inducement, the victim does not realize they are having intercourse; their consent is not a valid defense.

Penetration, no matter how slight, is the *actus reus* for rape.

At common law, a husband could not be guilty of raping his spouse.

The underage participant in intercourse cannot be found guilty as a conspirator to commit statutory rape or as an accessory to statutory rape.

In most jurisdictions, the mistake of the underage participant's age is not a defense to statutory rape.

A mistake of age is a defense to the crime of attempted statutory rape.

Kidnapping

Two elements to simple kidnapping:

> false imprisonment, and

> asportation (carrying away).

Demand for a ransom is a necessary element of aggravated kidnapping but not an element of simple kidnapping.

For the false imprisonment element of kidnapping, the perpetrator must confine the victim against their will, and the victim must be aware of the confinement.

Any movement of the victim of false imprisonment without their consent from the place where imprisoned satisfies the asportation element of kidnapping.

Property Crimes

Common law theft crimes

The three common law theft crimes are:

larceny

embezzlement

obtaining property by false pretenses.

Since these crimes are mutually exclusive, many questions require distinguishing them.

Larceny requires a trespassory taking; the defendant cannot have the rightful possession when the property is removed from the victim.

Embezzlement is when the defendant had rightful possession when the conversion occurred.

Obtaining property by *false pretenses* occurs when the defendant obtains the property's title and possession due to a fraudulent act.

Larceny

Larceny is the trespassory taking and asportation (carrying-away) of another's personal property, with the intent to deprive the possessor of the property permanently.

An intent to destroy the property is equivalent to permanently deprive the possessor.

Any movement of the property of another, no matter how slight, satisfies the asportation element of larceny.

The specific intent necessary for larceny (i.e., to permanently deprive the person entitled to possession of the property) is missing if the defendant intended to return the property when they committed the trespassory taking.

If the property is unintentionally destroyed while in possession of a defendant who took it with the intent to return it, the defendant is not guilty of larceny.

If the defendant does not intend to steal because they mistakenly think, either reasonably or unreasonably, that the property belongs to them, they are not guilty of larceny.

The trespassory taking element of larceny is satisfied if an innocent agent takes the property at the defendant's direction.

A person holding title to property can be guilty of larceny if they wrongfully take that property from a person entitled to possession of it.

If a lower-level employee is in physical possession of their employer's property, the employee only has custody of it.

Embezzlement

Embezzlement is completed when a person in rightful possession of property converts it to their use to permanently deprive the property owner.

Without "possession" of the goods, the crime is larceny, not embezzlement.

An offer to return the property later does not negate the crime.

Embezzlement only occurs when the defendant in rightful possession of the personal property of another converts it to their use.

If a defendant converts property to their use and intends to steal, they are guilty of the crime of larceny, not embezzlement.

If a bailee, who has possession of the totality of the goods entrusted to them by the bailor, breaks into the container holding goods and takes a portion, they are deemed only to have custody of the goods taken.

Obtaining property by false pretenses

To constitute the crime of obtaining property by false pretenses:

1) There must be a false material fact.

2) The defendant must know that it is false; an honest but unreasonable belief that the statement is true is not enough to constitute guilt.

3) The victim must rely on the statement of material fact.

4) The defendant must obtain title to the property. If the property is cash and is deliberately delivered to the defendant, the defendant's possession would equal title.

5) The defendant must intend to deprive the victim of the property permanently.

An honest belief in the truth of the defendant's representation, even if that belief is unreasonable, negates the specific intent necessary for the crime of obtaining property by false pretenses.

Larceny by trick

Larceny by trick is a form of larceny which occurs when the defendant obtains possession of the property by fraud.

Since the defendant does not have rightful possession of the property when they form the intent to steal, there is a trespassory taking, and the crime is known as larceny by trick.

Even though the defendant has physical possession of the property, this is not a conversion from one in possession, so the crime is not embezzlement.

Receiving stolen goods

A belief, either reasonable or unreasonable that the goods possessed by the defendant were not stolen is a defense to the crime of receiving stolen goods.

The property must have the characteristic of being "stolen goods" when the defendant possesses them for a conviction to occur.

If goods, once stolen, are recovered by the police, restored to their rightful owners, and offered to a defendant, the defendant cannot be convicted of receiving stolen goods.

Robbery

The underlying crimes of larceny or attempted larceny are essential elements of the crimes of robbery and attempted robbery.

For the crime to be robbery and not larceny, the trespassory taking must occur from the person through force or intimidation.

The element "from the person" means property within the person's control.

The force and intimidation must coincide with the larceny.

If all elements of robbery are present, the underlying crime of larceny and (if present) the underlying crimes of assault and battery merge into the crime of robbery.

If the defendant has stolen property, the use of force or intimidation to retain possession of it does not constitute the crime of robbery.

The threat to use force in the future and obtaining property through the use of that threat is the crime of extortion, not robbery.

The victim must be intimidated for the crime to be robbery.

Burglary

Common law burglary is defined as breaking and entering the *dwelling of another* (burglary cannot be committed in your own house) in the *nighttime* to *commit a felony therein*.

Modern statutes redefined burglary to eliminate the nighttime requirement and include all buildings.

The breaking and the entering elements of burglary need not coincide.

To be guilty of burglary, the defendant must have the specific intent to commit a felony on the premises at the moment of the entering. There is no requirement for the intended felony to be successful.

If a person enters through an open door, the breaking element of burglary is not present.

Burglary is committed if the defendant breaks and enters a dwelling house, even if the defendant does not break when they first enter the dwelling.

Breaking and entering need not occur by force.

If the defendant obtains entry to the property through fraud, the breaking and entering elements are present.

Since the common law definition of burglary requires that the property be the dwelling house of another, a person cannot commit burglary by breaking and entering their own home.

There is no breaking when entering through an open window/door or when the premises are open to the public.

A defendant in a space open to the public can be guilty of burglary if they break and enter into an adjoining space not open to the public.

There is no breaking and entering if the defendant opens personal property (e.g., a chest) while the property is open to the public.

A defendant is not guilty of burglary if committing larceny on premises open to the public.

If the original entry to the property was not breaking and entering, the defendant could be guilty of burglary if they break into a portion of the real estate once on the premises.

A defendant is not guilty of burglary by entering a commercial establishment while open to the public, hiding until after closing time, stealing, and breaking out of the property.

Arson

At common law, arson is the intentional burning of the dwelling house of another.

The definition has statutorily been expanded to the burning of a building, including one's own dwelling house, to defraud an insurer.

Arson has been committed if an act was done under circumstances where there was a direct and strong likelihood that a fire would result even if the defendant did not desire it, or if the fire resulted from reckless conduct by the defendant.

Since the common law definition of arson requires that the property involved be the dwelling house of another, a defendant cannot commit common law arson by burning their house.

Most jurisdictions have enacted statutes to include burning one's home as arson.

For the defendant to be guilty of arson, there must be combustion of a portion of real property.

The burning of personal property alone is insufficient to constitute arson.

Starting a fire accidentally does not constitute the *mens rea* for arson.

However, if the defendant lets an accidental fire continue to burn even though they could have easily put it out, the decision to let it burn is sufficient *mens rea* for arson.

Forgery

Forgery is the fraudulent making of false writings that have legal significance.

Notes for active learning

Inchoate Crimes

An inchoate (i.e., incomplete) crime is preparing to commit another crime (e.g., attempt).

Attempts

A person cannot be guilty of the crime of *attempt to commit* a crime unless they intend to commit the crime.

This applies to crimes, including strict liability offenses, where intent to commit the completed crime is not required.

The crime of attempt merges with the substantive crime if the defendant completes the substantive crime.

If the act which the defendant intends to perpetrate is not a crime, they cannot be guilty of attempt at any stage of their action, even if they think their act is a crime and intends to be engaged in criminal conduct.

An attempt requires substantial preparation to commit a substantive crime. Substantial preparation requires proximity to the place and time of the execution of the target crime.

Attempt is likely to be found where the acts required for the crime have been completed.

Attempt is likely to be found where the defendant has progressed so far that they would be unlikely to stop without outside interference.

Factual impossibility is a defense to an attempted crime if and only if the defendant did not know that the commission of the crime was inherently impossible.

Conspiracy

Conspiracy is defined as an agreement by two or more individuals for an unlawful purpose.

The agreement among conspirators necessary for that combination can be inferred from the parties' actions and need not be expressed.

To be a conspirator, a defendant must intend to agree with other conspirators and intend to accomplish the conspiracy objective.

Conspiracy is a separate crime from the substantive offense; the object of the conspiracy.

The crime of conspiracy does not merge with that substantive offense if the conspiracy accomplishes its objective.

A conspiracy is a completed crime at common law, even if no conspirator has committed an overt act in pursuance of the conspiracy.

The crime is not complete under federal law until an overt act occurs.

At common law, a conspiracy starts at the time of the agreement.

In a jurisdiction in which there must be an overt act to complete the crime of conspiracy, the conspiracy commences when the overt act takes place.

The conspiracy ends when the conspiracy objectives are accomplished or when abandoned.

A person who is a conspirator is guilty not only of the crime of conspiracy but of substantive crimes committed by co-conspirators according to the conspiracy if they are within the scope of the conspiracy and are committed while the conspiracy existed.

To be guilty of conspiracy, the defendant must combine with at least one other who is not necessary to the substantive crime to commit an unlawful or lawful act by unlawful means.

There must be as many conspirators as there are persons needed to commit the substantive offense plus one.

Ordinarily, two or more persons are needed for the crime of conspiracy.

For example, if two persons are needed to commit the substantive crime (e.g., the crime of adultery), there must be three conspirators.

A member of a legislatively protected class (e.g., a minor involved in statutory rape) cannot be counted as a conspirator.

If all possible conspirators other than the defendant are acquitted of conspiracy, the defendant must be acquitted.

A person who has committed the crime of conspiracy is not guilty of the other conspirators' substantive crimes if they *withdraw* from the conspiracy before the substantive crimes are committed.

To *withdraw* from the conspiracy, a conspirator must disaffirm the conspiracy's goals and inform the co-conspirators of the withdrawal.

Withdrawal is not a defense to the conspiracy crime.

If persons combine to perform a lawful act, they are not guilty of conspiracy even if they believe that the act they are to perform is illegal.

The impossibility of accomplishing the purpose of the conspiracy is not a defense to the crime of conspiracy.

A person is guilty of conspiracy only if they intend to join with another to commit a crime.

Solicitation

The act of asking another person to commit a crime with the intent that the person asked should commit that crime is a sufficient *actus reus* and *mens rea* for the crime of solicitation.

Once a person solicited agrees to commit the crime, there is a conspiracy between the solicitor and the person solicited.

The crime of solicitation is merged into the conspiracy so that the solicitor is no longer guilty of conspiracy.

Parties to crimes

The person who knows that the principal is committing a crime and intends to help the principal is guilty as an accomplice.

A person, even though they intend to help with the commission of an illegal act, is not guilty as an accessory if the act which they are helping the principal commit is, in fact, not a criminal act.

Presence at the crime scene without assisting or encouraging the principal does not incur accomplice liability.

If a person present at a crime scene encourages the principal to commit the criminal act, they are guilty as an accomplice.

Supplying goods or services which have criminal and non-criminal uses to a person, with the knowledge that they will be used in a crime, can cause the supplier to be guilty of accomplice liability.

Supplying goods that can only be used for criminal purposes without precise knowledge of their intended use can be the basis for accomplice liability if the recipient uses those goods to commit a crime.

An essential element of the crime of accessory after the fact is that the defendant must have aided the felon to hinder the felon's capture or conviction.

Notes for active learning

General intent crimes

There must be a coincidence of the intent to accomplish the *actus reus* with the actual accomplishment of the *actus reus* for a defendant to be guilty of a general intent crime.

Intent for criminal law is when a person desires a result, and that result occurs.

Intent is present even though the person thought the end would be accomplished by different means.

Specific intent crimes

To be guilty of a specific intent crime, the defendant must have the required specific intent, which is more than an attempt to accomplish the *actus reus* when accomplishing the *actus reus*.

For example, in the specific intent crime of larceny, the defendant must have the intent to deprive the possessor of their property when they engage in the trespassory taking.

The mental state of maliciousness is associated with an intentional act, but it can be present where the defendant acts recklessly.

Strict liability

If a statute does not include language requiring fault, a court may impose liability without fault (i.e., strict liability) after considering factors, such as:

> legislative history,

> severity of the punishment for the crime,

> seriousness of harm to the public created by the criminal activity,

> defendant's opportunities to be informed of the facts which lead to an offense,

> difficulty of proving *mens rea*,

> number of violations,

> likelihood that prosecution is likely to occur.

No mental state is required for the defendant to be guilty of a strict liability offense.

A defendant is guilty of strict liability if they accomplish the *actus reus*.

A principal can be guilty of a strict liability offense for an act performed by their agent, which is within the scope of authority.

Specifically, forbidding such an agent to perform an illegal act is not a defense.

To be guilty of an attempt to commit a strict liability offense (distinguished from the guilt of the crime itself), the defendant must have the specific intent to commit the offense.

Mistake of fact and law

Neither a mistake of law nor a mistake of fact, whether reasonable or unreasonable, is a defense to a strict liability offense.

A reasonable mistake of fact is a defense to a general intent crime.

Neither a mistake of law nor an unreasonable mistake of fact is a defense to a general intent crime.

A reasonable and unreasonable mistake of fact and a mistake of law that prevent the specific intent from being formed are valid defenses to a specific intent crime.

If a crime requires the specific intent of "knowing," and the defendant subjectively does not know that their actions are criminal because they relied on the erroneous advice of a lawyer, the defendant is not guilty of the crime.

Insanity

If the individual knows what they are doing and knows that it is a crime, delusions caused by mental illness will not establish the defense of insanity under the *M'Naghten* test.

The *M'Naghten* test of insanity does *not* include the irresistible impulse test.

Intoxication

Generally, voluntary intoxication is not a defense to a crime.

However, if voluntary intoxication prevents the specific intent necessary for a specific intent crime from being formed, the defendant is not guilty of the specific intent crime.

If the crime of first-degree murder requires deliberate premeditation and voluntary intoxication prevents the defendant from premeditating, the defendant would be guilty of second-degree murder.

Causation

If the defendant sets in motion actions that cause the victim's death, the fact that the victim would have died sooner if they had not set those actions in motion is not a defense to the homicide crime.

A defendant is not guilty of murder, even though they inflict serious bodily harm, which will eventually result in death if the victim dies from an independent cause.

If a defendant inflicts serious bodily harm on the victim, which would not cause death if the victim received proper medical treatment, the defendant is guilty of murder when the victim dies from their injury due to lack of proper medical treatment.

The improper medical treatment is not an independent cause relieving the defendant of liability.

Justification

A police officer is not criminally liable if they used deadly force to apprehend a person when they reasonably believe that they are committing or escaping from a dangerous felony.

A police officer is not justified in using deadly force to arrest a person for a non-dangerous felony or a misdemeanor.

A person who assists a police officer in apprehending a criminal has the same right to use force as the police officer they are assisting.

Notes for active learning

Constitutional Protections

Arrest

An arrest warrant is required to validly arrest an individual in their home, except if the arrest occurs while the arresting officer was in *hot pursuit*.

If the person commits a misdemeanor in a police officer's presence, the officer has the right to arrest without a warrant.

A police officer who has a reasonable belief that a person has committed a felony has the right to arrest without a warrant at any place except in the defendant's home.

The fact that the defendant was unlawfully arrested is not a defense to subsequent criminal prosecution for the offense for which they were arrested.

However, evidence seized as the result of an unlawful arrest is inadmissible in court.

Definition of a search

Only searches by governmental authorities, persons acting as agents, or under their direction and control, are governed by the Fourth and Fourteenth Amendments' exclusionary rule.

The exclusionary rule does not foreclose evidence obtained by searches by private parties.

Searches that require warrants or an exception to the warrant requirements to be valid are closely tied to the concept of a reasonable expectation of privacy.

While a homeowner has a reasonable expectation of privacy from ground-level intrusion in the fenced-in backyard of their home, they have no reasonable expectation of privacy from aerial surveillance.

A homeowner is protected from searches by advanced devices measuring heat escaping from their home.

The person, desk file, and file cabinets in a private office at work, a changing room in a clothing store, and containers of personal effects are protected areas.

An individual does not have a reasonable expectation of privacy in open fields beyond the home's curtilage. Warrantless searches beyond the curtilage of homes are permitted.

The government can obtain financial records in the custody of banks, accountants, or other third parties by a subpoena on the third party without obtaining a search warrant.

There is no search and seizure if the object taken is in plain view from a place where the law enforcement agent has a lawful right to be.

Search procedure – standing

An individual only has standing to object to searches that violate their reasonable expectation of privacy, not that of third persons.

Ordinarily, the claimant must show a possessory interest in the items seized and a legitimate expectation of privacy in the areas searched.

A search's validity cannot be challenged in a grand jury proceeding.

The proper way to raise the validity of a search is by a pre-trial motion to suppress.

An objection to the admission of improperly seized evidence at trial is available only when the search facts are unknown to the defendant beforehand.

A defendant has the right to establish standing without admitting the seized evidence was under their control and without that admission being admissible at trial.

A guest in a home has standing to challenge a search of that home.

Search incident to a valid arrest

The police may search a defendant's person and the area in their immediate control incident to a valid arrest.

To protect safety, police may, incident to a lawful arrest, search the premises in which the arrest took place to find other persons who may have been present and involved in the crime.

The search must immediately follow or be contemporaneous with the arrest.

Objects seized in a warrantless search made according to an invalid arrest are inadmissible.

Objects seized in a search before there is a valid ground to make an arrest are inadmissible unless there is another ground than a search incident to an arrest to justify their admissibility.

Consent searches

Consent must be by either the owner or the person entrusted with the property.

A person other than the defendant can give valid consent to search areas over which they have access jointly with the defendant.

Consent obtained by fraud or duress is invalid.

The consent given by an individual to search their property must be voluntary, but the suspect need not be warned that they do not have to consent.

The superintendent of an apartment house complex or the manager of a hotel does not have the authority to validly consent to the search of an apartment or room in a hotel rented to persons occupying the premises.

Automobile searches

There is a lesser expectation of privacy in a motor vehicle than in a person's home, and therefore greater latitude to permit warrantless searches.

A non-owner passenger does not have standing to object to the search of an automobile.

If police engage in the random stopping and searching of motor vehicles, the search is invalid.

The police may conduct a valid search of vehicles at a fixed checkpoint, at the border, or the functional equivalent of a border.

If the police have probable cause to stop a motor vehicle, including a stop for a traffic violation, the police may validly search the automobile (including the trunk and containers in the automobile) without a warrant.

The search need not take place immediately. If the motor vehicle is impounded, the police may conduct an inventory search.

Regulatory search

A regulatory search may be made without a warrant, even if the search is to obtain evidence of criminal activity.

Regulatory searches are confined to businesses and premises that must be licensed to operate legally (e.g., gambling establishments, businesses serving alcoholic beverages) and businesses selling merchandise where criminal activity is likely (e.g., pawn shops).

Other warrantless searches

A "stop and frisk" pat-down search is constitutionally valid even if there are no grounds for a valid arrest, as long as there is reasonable suspicion of criminal behavior.

The search is limited to a "pat-down" search but may be extended to a more intrusive search if the *pat-down* uncovers an object which reasonably could be a weapon.

A search of school lockers without a warrant is permissible.

Searches under a search warrant

Police or anther investigatory agencies may not issue a search warrant.

A search warrant may only be issued by a judge or other neutral magistrate based upon probable cause set forth in the warrant application.

The application for a search warrant does not require independent evidence on the basis for the search and the reliability of the informant.

The magistrate can issue a valid warrant based upon the totality of the circumstances.

The application for the search warrant must state, with particularity, the place to be searched and the objects of the search.

If, when executing the warrant, the police find evidence not explicitly mentioned in the warrant, they may validly seize it.

If the application for a search warrant is not sufficient to establish probable cause, but the magistrate nevertheless grants a search warrant, and the police execute it believing in good faith that the search warrant is valid, the property seized according to the search is admissible.

If the police are granted a search warrant based upon information that they know is false, evidence obtained according to that warrant is inadmissible because the search is invalid.

Fruits of an illegal search

If a search is illegal and information obtained from that illegal search is used to conduct further searches that would otherwise be proper or to obtain admissions from a defendant, which they would otherwise not have obtained, the information or the evidence obtained will be excluded from evidence as *the fruits of an illegal search*.

Coerced confessions

If either the police or a private individual obtains a confession or admission by coercion (either physical or psychological), the statement made is inadmissible for any purpose.

This rule against admission by coercion applies even if the defendant was given the Miranda warning and waived it.

If a coerced confession is improperly admitted, the conviction will not be overturned on appeal if the admission of the confession constitutes a harmless error.

Miranda warning

The *Miranda warning* is applicable only when there is interrogation by the police while the defendant is in custody.

An individual is in custody if their freedom to leave the police's presence is restricted.

A statement made to a private individual not working in concert with the police is not subject to Miranda rights limitations.

Volunteered statements are not the products of interrogation.

If the police engage in conduct other than questioning the defendant designed to elicit a statement, that statement is considered the product of interrogation.

Statements made by a defendant in custody due to interrogation are inadmissible at a subsequent trial unless the defendant is informed of Miranda rights and waives them.

If the defendant exercises their Miranda rights by demanding a lawyer, statements made in response to questioning after that demand and before a lawyer is present are inadmissible.

Further questioning can occur only after the defendant consults with their lawyer and agrees to further questions.

A statement given in violation of the defendant's Miranda rights is admissible to impeach their credibility if they take the stand in their trial and testify in a manner inconsistent with the statement previously given.

If the defendant exercises their Miranda right to remain silent while in custody, that silence in the face of accusations made to them that they committed the crime cannot be used in the trial as an adoptive admission.

The police need not inform the defendant of the charge they are investigating to obtain a valid waiver of Miranda rights.

If a defendant waives their Miranda rights and agrees to submit to interrogation, they may be questioned about more subjects than the crime, which is the primary object of the police interrogation.

Once a defendant is indicted or otherwise formally charged with a crime, the right to counsel accrues. The defendant cannot be interrogated by the police except in the presence of counsel, even if given Miranda warnings and waived their Miranda rights.

Lineups and other forms of identification

A right to counsel at a lineup only after the criminal process (i.e., indictment) has occurred.

The fact of a lineup identification without counsel present after an indictment is not admissible at trial, but the victim can still make an in-court identification.

Testimonies about lineup identification and subsequent in-court identification are inadmissible if the pre-trial identification offends due process standards.

Due process is violated when the likelihood of proper identification is so remote because the victim could not observe the criminal or because the lineup, whether pre-indictment or post-indictment, is very prejudicial.

Right to counsel

A conviction is invalid if the defendant has not had the opportunity for the assistance of counsel in the trial of felonies and misdemeanors for which the defendant is incarcerated, or the penalty on conviction includes the possibility of incarceration.

A defendant has the right to refuse to have counsel appointed and act as their lawyer.

If they act as their lawyer, they cannot later raise inadequacy of representation or being denied the right to counsel.

A defendant has the right to have counsel provided to prosecute only one appeal.

A defendant's conviction will be reversed even if they had a lawyer if the representation is ruled inadequate.

An attorney representing a defendant who represents a co-defendant may have a conflict of interest, which is so severe that they cannot render effective assistance of counsel.

Public trial

The public's right to a public trial can be enforced by the news media even if both prosecutor and defendant object.

The court has the discretion to ban or limit the public at a trial if there is a substantial likelihood of prejudice to the defendant or a need to limit access to ensure an orderly proceeding.

Fair conduct by the prosecutor

A prosecutor has an affirmative obligation to disclose to the defendant material known or in possession of the prosecutor's office, which is exculpatory.

Speedy trial

The beginning point to measure a defendant's right to a speedy trial is when criminal proceedings commence, not the time that the crime is committed.

The prosecution can wait until the day before the statute of limitations expires to indict and start the clock on the right to a speedy trial.

The passage of time alone does not give the defendant the right to dismissal for lack of a speedy trial.

The defendant must show prejudice from the delay.

Jury trial

In a criminal case, the defendant is entitled to a jury trial if the greatest possible sentence can exceed six months in jail.

The defendant is entitled to be tried by a jury chosen from a venire in which there is no systematic racial, ethnic, or gender exclusion.

There is a right to challenge the jury's racial makeup, even if the defendant is not a member of the race excluded.

When selecting a petit jury, neither the defendant nor the prosecutor may use peremptory challenges to systematically exclude individuals of one race or gender from the jury.

The state may constitutionally try a defendant before a petit jury, which contains no members of the defendant's minority group if the procedure for selecting the jury venire was proper. There was no systematic exclusion of jurors through the exercise of peremptory challenges.

A judge must take some procedural steps before accepting a guilty plea; otherwise, the plea will not satisfy the process standard that the plea is voluntary and intelligent.

The judge must inform the defendant that they:

> need not plead guilty,

> has a right to a jury trial.

The judge must explain:

1)   the elements of the crime with which the defendant is charged, and

2)   the maximum possible legal penalty.

Confrontation

The prosecution has satisfied the defendant's right to confront the witness if the witness appeared at a preliminary hearing where the defendant had the right to cross-examine, and there is a valid excuse for the witness's failure to appear at trial.

Then, the evidence given at the preliminary hearing is admissible under the prior testimony exception to the hearsay rule.

A criminal defendant does not have the Sixth Amendment constitutional right to confront their accuser at a preliminary hearing.

If the accuser is a child who might suffer substantial emotional damage by appearing in the same room as the defendant, the accused's right to confront the witness is satisfied by watching the testimony electronically.

Severance

When two individuals are charged with the same crime and one has given a confession that implicates the other, the non-confessing defendant has the right to have their trial severed from that of the confessing defendant unless the statements in the confession implicating the non-confessing defendant can be excised.

When a confession is admissible against the confessing defendant but is inadmissible against the non-confessing defendant, severance is not required under *Nelson v. O'Neil* (1971) if the confessing defendant testifies at trial because the non-confessing defendant has the right to cross-examine about the truthfulness of that confession.

Standard of proof

To satisfy its burden of proof in a criminal case, the prosecution must prove *all elements of the offense beyond a reasonable doubt.*

In a murder case, the burden of proof includes showing that the elements which would reduce murder to manslaughter are not present.

If state law so provides, the defendant can be given the obligation to plead affirmative defenses and prove them by a preponderance of the evidence.

Unless the state has shifted the burden of proof of insanity to the defendant, once a criminal defendant has raised the defense of insanity, the prosecution must prove that the defendant is sane beyond a reasonable doubt.

In a voluntary manslaughter prosecution, lack of justification is an element of the crime and must be proven by the prosecution beyond a reasonable doubt.

Imposition of the death penalty

A court can only order the death penalty if the defendant has committed murder.

When there is a felony murder where several conspirators participated in the felony, the death penalty can only be administered to the individual who caused the death.

A statute mandating the death penalty for a specific crime is unconstitutional because a jury must have the opportunity to impose the death penalty only after considering mitigating factors.

The death penalty can only be imposed by a jury.

A judge can not impose the death penalty after the jury has convicted the defendant of the substantive crime.

Fair trial – post-trial stage

The appellate court may constitutionally vacate a sentence and order a new trial if it determines that the verdict is against the weight of the evidence.

While the prosecution cannot, except in rebuttal, introduce a defendant's criminal record in a criminal trial, the judge can review the record for purposes of deciding the appropriate sentence.

Double jeopardy

Jeopardy attaches to the double jeopardy clause in a criminal jury trial when the jury is sworn.

In a jury-waived trial, the double jeopardy clause becomes operational when the first witness begins to testify.

The defendant does not have the defense of double jeopardy when the judge declares a mistrial to benefit the defendant or appellate court orders a new trial from the defendant's appeal.

The prosecution has the right to appeal a criminal judgment of not guilty only if the appeals court's judgment will have the right to reinstitute a guilty verdict, and there will be no new trial.

If a defendant is tried and convicted of a criminal offense of assault and battery, and the victim later dies, the defense of double jeopardy does not apply to a subsequent homicide prosecution for the death arising out of the acts which constituted the assault and battery.

The statute of limitations on criminal activity starts to run when the last act, an element of the crime, occurs.

Double jeopardy prevents prosecution in a subsequent case for any crime with an essential element of the crime prosecuted earlier.

Double jeopardy does not prevent prosecution for a crime that coincided with but was not an essential element of the crime which was first prosecuted.

Collateral estoppel

Under the collateral estoppel (issue preclusion) branch of the double jeopardy clause, the prosecution may not constitutionally litigate issues that have been litigated and decided in favor of the defendant in a previous criminal case.

Notes for active learning

Guilty Pleas and Plea Bargaining

Plea colloquy

The plea conversation between a judge and a criminal defendant has four requirements:

nature of the charge,

maximum authorized sentence and mandatory minimum,

defendant's right to plead not guilty and go to trial, and

by pleading guilty, a defendant is waiving trial, and the case proceeds to sentence.

The court must ask the defendant if they understand each of these points and receive a voluntary affirmative response.

Failure by the court to advise the defendant of any of the above supplies grounds for a collateral attack of the plea.

If such an attack is successful, the guilty plea will be withdrawn, and the defendant will be allowed to enter a new plea.

A defendant may withdraw a guilty plea after sentencing if:

problem with a colloquy,

jurisdictional defect,

defendant prevails if deprived of effective assistance of counsel, and

prosecutor fails to fulfill their agreement.

Fifth Amendment privilege against compelled testimony

Anyone can assert the privilege in *any* proceeding where an individual testifies under oath.

Must be asserted *at the first opportunity,* or else it is lost.

Privilege against compelled testimony:

protected from compelled testimony only, does not apply to the state's use of a person's biological samples, and

prosecutors cannot comment on the assertion of the privilege.

Eliminating privilege against compelled testimony

There are three methods to eliminate the privilege against compelled testimony.

1) Immunity grant for the use and derivative use of testimony. The prosecution cannot use the defendant's testimony, or anything derived from it to convict.

   However, a defendant can be convicted based on evidence obtained before a grant of immunity.

2) Defendant takes the stand and waives the Fifth Amendment right against self-incrimination as to anything properly within the scope of cross-examination.

3) The statute of limitations has run on the underlying crime because of no criminal prosecution.

Punishment

Eighth Amendment prohibits:

1) Criminal penalties *grossly* disproportionate to the seriousness of the offense.

2) Death penalty statute that creates an automatic category for imposition.

3) Juries must be allowed to hear *all potentially mitigating evidence.*

4) Death penalty *prohibited* for a mentally disabled person, presently insane or was under 18 at the time of the offense.

Criminal Law and Procedure – Quick Facts

1. **Attempting**, even *with* criminal intent, to do an act that is *not* itself a crime is *not* a conviction that is likely to be upheld.

2. **Larceny** – the **taking** and **asportation** (i.e., carrying away) of another's personal property by *trespass* and with **intent to permanently deprive** the person of their interest in the property.

   For example, the moving of a refrigerator (e.g., by salesclerk) to the loading dock constitutes a taking and carrying away; since the clerk did *not* have permission to move merchandise in this way, it was trespassory. Since the clerk intended to permanently deprive the store of an interest in the refrigerator when they moved it, their subsequent *change of heart* was **too late**.

3. The element of **carrying away** (i.e., **asportation**) is satisfied when there is a **movement** of the property as **a step** in carrying it away.

4. The **continuing trespass doctrine** renders continued possession of the property to be trespassory.

   So, if the trespasser later develops the intent to steal, the actions are considered **larceny**.

5. **Attempted murder** is a *specific intent* crime, though a defendant can be found guilty of murder when their actions demonstrate a very high degree of recklessness.

   If the charge is **attempted murder**, it *must* be shown that the defendant committed an act with the **intent** to kill someone.

6. The Fourth Amendment is *not* violated by a statute authorizing warrantless searches of a **probationer's home** with reasonable grounds to believe contraband is present.

7. If a statute is intended to **protect members of a limited class from exploitation**, members of that class are presumed to be immune from liability, even if they participated in the crime in a manner that would otherwise make them liable.

8. The defendant has a legitimate defense where the **statute** under which charged was *not* **published or made reasonably available** before the conduct.

9. For an **affirmative defense** (e.g., insanity), it is permissible to impose the **burden of proof on the defendant**.

10. **Larceny by trick** occurs when property **possession** is obtained by **misrepresentation.**

11. **Pretenses** are the appropriate offense when the misrepresentations have prompted the victim to **convey title** of the property to the defendant.

Relationship matrix

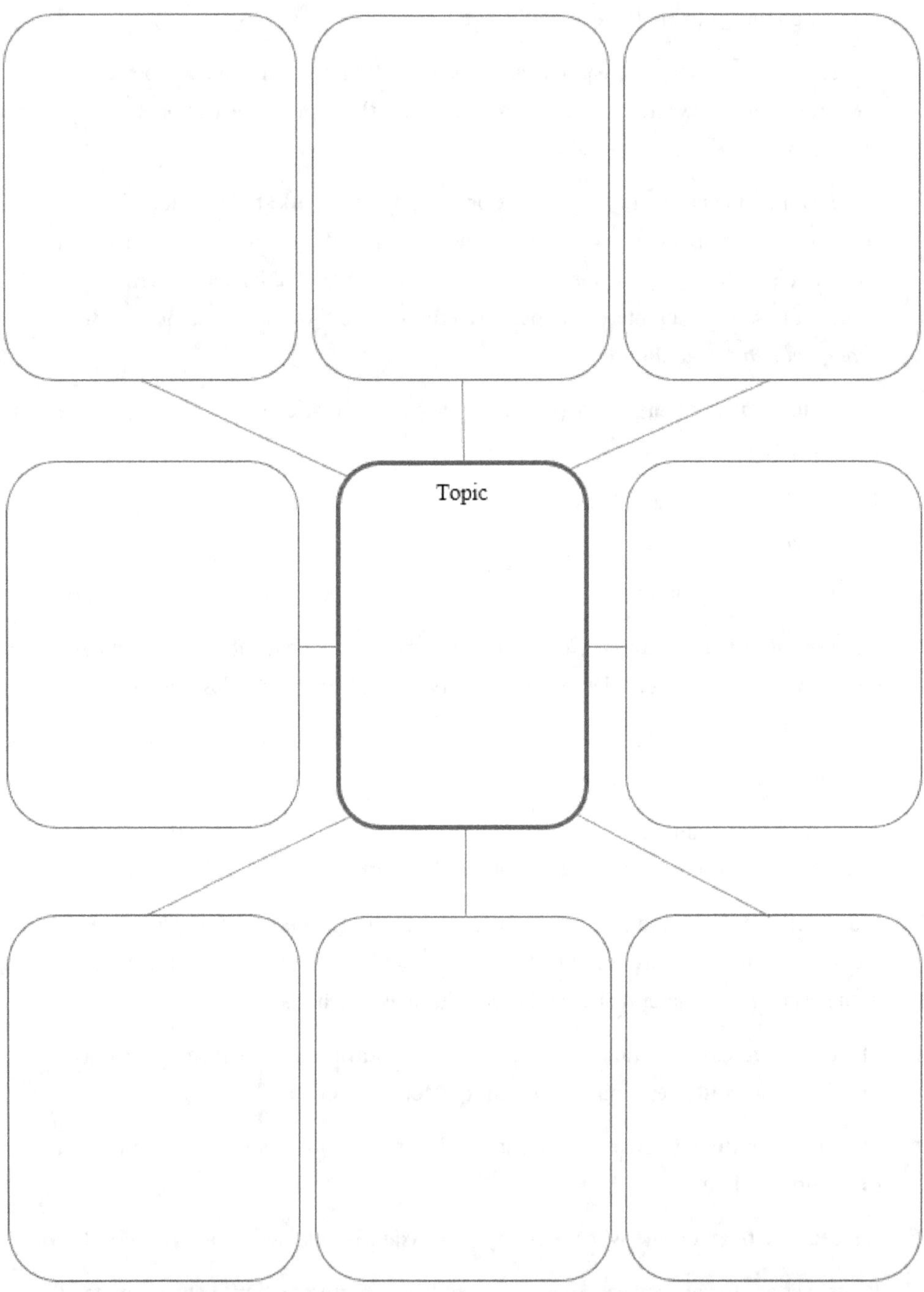

Notes for active learning

Notes for active learning

Review Questions

Multiple-choice questions

1. A criminal conviction requires a:

   A. Magnanimous jury vote   **C.** Divided jury vote

   B. Hung jury vote   **D.** Unanimous jury vote

2. A plurality decision means:

   A. A majority cannot agree as to the outcome of the case

   B. A agree with the majority outcome, but not with the reasoning

   C. A tie vote is cast

   D. None of the above

3. The RICO statute was created in response to:

   A. Corrupt politicians   **C.** Recidivist criminals

   B. Organized crime   **D.** Illegal immigration

4. Battered women's syndrome may prove self-defense in homicide cases where:

   A. The defendant is especially grieved and remorseful

   B. The woman accused of killing her husband, with evidence of sustained violence

   C. The victim was not well-liked or respected in the community

   D. None of the above

5. Criminal laws in the United States are enacted by:

   I. Federal government

   II. State governments

   III. Municipal governments

   A. I only   **C.** III only

   B. I and II only   **D.** I, II and III

6. When two or more persons agree to commit a crime, that is a:

   A. Bribe   **C.** Plea Bargain

   B. Contract   **D.** Conspiracy

7. A person charged with a crime in the United States is:

A. Presumed guilty

B. Presumed innocent until proven guilty

C. Presumed not-guilty

D. None of the above

8. Warrantless Searches are allowed when:

I. Incident to an arrest

II. The evidence is in plain view

III. The evidence is likely to be destroyed

A. I only

B. I and II only

C. I and III only

D. I, II and III

9. The following may be imposed for a crime:

I. Imposition of a fine

II. Imprisonment

III. Retribution

A. I only

B. I and II only

C. II only

D. I, II and III

10. The protection against self-incrimination does not apply to:

I. Body fluids

II. Corporations

III. Testimony

A. I only

B. I and II only

C. III only

D. I, II and III

11. *Actus reus* indicates:

A. Guilty mind

B. Criminal intent

C. Guilty act

D. None of the above

12. The Eighth Amendment prohibits:

A. Electrocution capital punishment

B. Sterilization

C. Life imprisonment without parole

D. Imprisonment in isolation

13. *Mens rea* indicates:

    I. Purposeful

    II. Knowingly

    III. Recklessly

A. I and II only   **C.** II and III only

B. I and III only   **D.** I, II and III

14. At the arraignment proceeding, the accused may plead:

    I. Guilty

    II. Not-guilty

    III. *Nolo-contendere*

A. I only   **C.** III only

B. I and II only   **D.** I, II and III

15. Crimes can be classified as:

    I. Felonies

    II. Misdemeanors

    III. Violations

A. I only   **C.** I and III only

B. I and II only   **D.** I, II and III

True/false questions

16. The United States has one of the most advanced and humane criminal law systems.

    True   False

17. In a criminal lawsuit, a private party is usually the plaintiff.

    True   False

18. Money laundering uses the proceeds of illegal activities and passing them through a legitimate business.

    True   False

19. *Specific intent* is where the accused acted unintentionally.

    True   False

20. Bribery is a white-collar crime.

> True   False

21. Most modern forms of burglary include threatening the victim with force, in addition to using force on the victim.

> True   False

22. The burden of proof is on the defendant to show they are not guilty.

> True   False

23. The defendant is formally charged in court at the indictment.

> True   False

24. Criminal charges may be brought even though the act was accidental.

> True   False

25. Most crimes require *mens rea* and *actus reus*.

> True   False

26. *Mala prohibita* crimes are those that are inherently evil.

> True   False

27. A penal code is found in a jurisdiction's statutes.

> True   False

28. Misdemeanors include crimes that are *mala in se*.

> True   False

29. The extortion of private persons is called blackmail.

> True   False

30. Misdemeanors are less serious crimes than felonies.

> True   False

31. For purposes of the SEC's rules, an insider includes an employee at any company level.

> True   False

Answer keys

1: D	11: C
2: B	12: B
3: B	13: D
4: B	14: D
5: D	15: D
6: D	
7: B	
8: D	
9: D	
10: B	

16: True	26: False
17: False	27: True
18: True	28: False
19: False	29: True
20: True	30: True
21: False	31: True
22: False	
23: False	
24: False	
25: True	

Notes for active learning

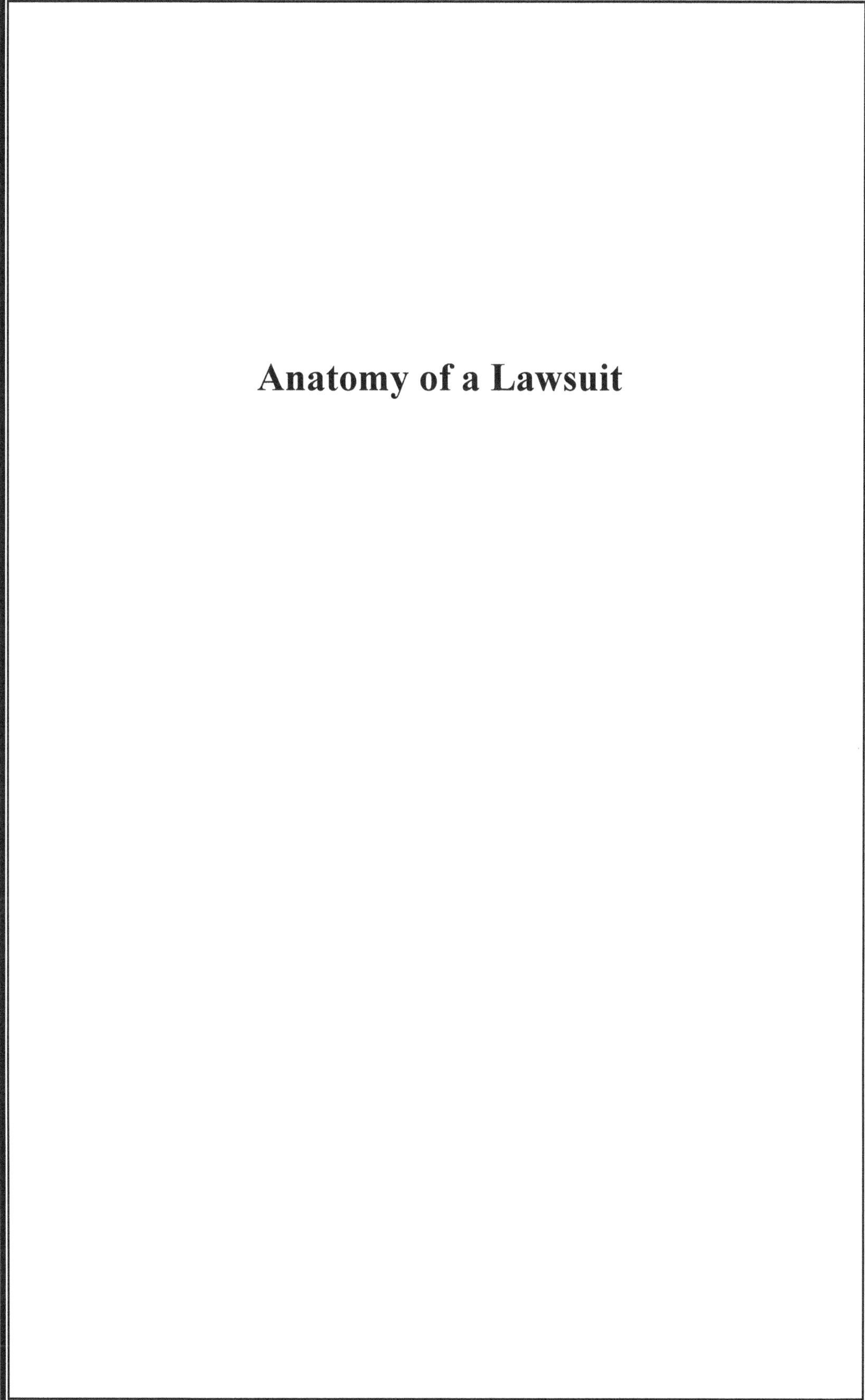

Anatomy of a Lawsuit

The Trial Process Overview

A lawsuit is a complicated legal process, whether suing, being sued, or acting as a witness. The legal process can have numerous unpleasant surprises and frustrating delays.

There are at least two parties to every action, and the court dictates the schedule and events. Some things happen in the same order in most litigation; the following chronology shows how a lawsuit proceeds. The actions may be different because of variations between state laws and rules of civil procedure.

At the start of a lawsuit, the legal papers filed in court are the pleadings (i.e., formal declarations of facts, claims, and the relief sought). Several documents become a part of a lawsuit, with some states have different names for the documents.

There are four main stages to a trial:

Pleading stage - filing the complaint and the defense's motions.

Pretrial stage - discovery process and finding of facts.

Trial stage - empaneling the jury, testimony on behalf of the plaintiffs, and testimony on behalf of the defendants.

Post-trial stage - concluding arguments, judge's charge to the jury, jury deliberations, announcement of judgment, motions for new trial or appeal.

Civil cases

A civil case begins when the plaintiff (i.e., person or entity) claims that the defendant (e.g., another person or entity) failed to perform a legal duty owed to the plaintiff. The plaintiff and the defendant are referred to as "parties" or "litigants." The plaintiff may ask the court to tell the defendant to fulfill the duty (i.e., performance) or make compensation (i.e., damages) for the harm done. Legal duties include respecting rights established under the Constitution, federal or state law.

For example, a lumberyard enters a contract to sell a specific amount of wood to a carpenter for an agreed-upon price. It fails to deliver the wood, forcing the carpenter to buy it elsewhere at a higher price. The carpenter might sue the lumberyard to pay the extra costs (i.e., damages) incurred because the lumberyard failed to deliver.

If these parties were from different states, that suit could be brought in federal court under diversity jurisdiction if the amount in question exceeded the minimum required by statute ($75,000.01).

Individuals, corporations, and the federal government can bring civil suits in federal court, claiming federal statutes or constitutional rights violations.

For example, the federal government can sue a hospital for overbilling Medicare and Medicaid, violating a federal statute. An individual could sue a local police department for violating their constitutional rights (e.g., the right to assemble peacefully).

Criminal cases

A person accused of a crime is generally charged in a formal accusation called an indictment (for felonies or serious crimes) or information (for misdemeanors). *On behalf of the people*, the government prosecutes the case through the United States Attorney's Office if the person is charged with a federal crime or the state's attorney's office (or district attorney) to prosecute state crimes.

It is not the victim's responsibility (nor right) to bring a criminal case. For example, the government would prosecute the kidnapper in a kidnapping case, and the victim would not be a party to the action. In some criminal cases, there may not be a specific victim. For example, state governments arrest and prosecute people accused of violating laws against driving while intoxicated because society regards that as a severe offense that can harm others.

When a court determines that an individual committed a crime, that person will receive a sentence. The sentence may be an order to pay a monetary penalty (e.g., restitution to the victim), imprisonment, supervision in the community, or some combination.

Intersection of civil and criminal cases

Civil cases involve disputes between (usually) private parties, while criminal cases are considered acts against the local or federal government. However, some acts may result in civil claims and criminal charges. For instance, a person may be sued for the intentional tort of assault or battery and may be arrested and charged with the crime of assault and battery.

There are times when a criminal act may give way to civil liability, such as when someone is charged with homicide and sued for wrongful death (typically follows the completion of the criminal trial). The criminal charges are punishable by fines, prison time, and other penalties, while the civil lawsuit focuses on recovering money to compensate the victim (or the victim's family) for damages.

The complaint initiates a lawsuit

A civil action (as opposed to a criminal or family proceeding, for example) begins with a *complaint*, usually accompanied by a *summons*. A complaint is a legal document that lays out the plaintiff's claims (the person bringing the lawsuit) has against the defendant (the person or business being sued).

The complaint (or *petition*) is the first document filed, which outlines the plaintiff's claims against the defendant. The complaint identifies the parties, sets the legal basis for the court's jurisdiction over the controversy, states the plaintiff's legal claims, relates the facts giving rise to the claims, and sets forth the plaintiff's request for relief. The plaintiff sets forth what they want the court to require the defendant to do, such as pay damages.

The complaint provides the defendant with notice of the factual and legal basis of the plaintiff's claims. Generally, the facts outlined in the complaint are based on the plaintiff's knowledge. The plaintiff may use the phrase "upon information and belief" for facts. The plaintiff may have learned about some facts from others and has formed a good-faith belief that the events are as described.

Most states require that the complaint set forth a *short and plain* statement of the plaintiff's claims. Often, the facts in the complaint are sparse and do not describe all events.

Summons

The summons is an order from the court where the lawsuit will be heard (i.e., litigated). The summons notifies the recipient (defendant) that they have been sued, refers to the complaint (or petition), and sets the time limit within which the defendant must file an answer or seek to have the case dismissed.

The summons describes the consequences of failing to respond promptly. For example, the case may be decided without the defendant, and the decision binds them. In jurisdictions where an action is commenced by service, the action can go on for a long time before the court ever becomes involved.

Failing to respond to a lawsuit on time causes the defendant to be *in default*.

Notice and service of process

The summons is delivered or *served* on the defendant along with the complaint. The summons is usually a form document with a preprinted caption that contains the name of the court, the parties, and a docket number (i.e., the court's identification number). The document informs the defendant that they have been sued; it serves as the *notice*.

Receipt is when somebody confirms their identity or mailed to the defendant; the *service of process.*

The summons, properly served, gives the court power (i.e., jurisdiction) over the dispute and the defendant. The court must have jurisdiction over the parties and issue described in the complaint. The decisions affecting the defendant are binding and enforceable for the litigated controversy.

Answer to the complaint

The defendant's response to the complaint is an *answer*, though some states use a different word. The answer addresses each paragraph in the complaint, and each response will ordinarily take one of three forms: "admitted," "denied," "insufficient knowledge to admit or deny." The answer says what portions of the complaint, if any, the defendant admits to, what the defendant contests, what defenses the defendant may have, and whether the defendant has claims against the plaintiff or others.

An answer may set forth various affirmative defenses, which are legal reasons why the defendant should not be held liable for the plaintiff's damages. Some of these defenses may be the basis of a motion to dismiss. The defendant must answer within a specific time (usually within weeks). If the defendant does not answer the complaint, the court may enter a default judgment.

Following the defendant's response to the plaintiffs' claims, the parties can choose to settle or request a judgment based on the evidence presented, or the court can decide to continue toward resolving the conflict at trial. If there is no judgment rendered, the case proceeds to the pretrial stage.

Counterclaim

If a defendant has a claim against the plaintiff, which arose out of the same circumstances as those that led to the complaint, it should be raised in the answer in a section entitled *counterclaims*. The counterclaim is written like the complaint.

If a defendant asserts a counterclaim in the answer, the plaintiff may respond by filing a *reply*. The reply admits, denies, or asserts that the plaintiff lacks information, just as the original answer did. The reply may assert defenses, just as the answer did.

Crossclaims

Crossclaims arise when two or more parties to the lawsuit, who are "aligned" as plaintiffs or defendants, have their dispute arising out of the same transaction or occurrence. A crossclaim is a claim against a party on the same side of an action.

Rule 13(g) of the Federal Rules of Civil Procedure, a crossclaim must be related to the original action in that it arises from the same transaction or occurrence as the original action or a counterclaim or involves property subject matter of the original action.

The person being sued in a crossclaim file an answer like the original complaint. For example, if Driver B and Driver C are sued by Driver A after a multiple-vehicle accident, and Driver C was injured by something Driver B did, Driver C might file a crossclaim against Driver B within the same lawsuit. The defendant will want to consider the various defenses available to them concerning the claim.

Third-party complaint

Sometimes a defendant who has been sued will have a legal reason for passing liability off to another person. This person may be brought into the lawsuit if the defendant files a third-party complaint. An example is a contract where the third party promises to pay another if the defendant is found liable.

The complaint sets forth the facts giving rise to the defendant's claim against the third party and requests relief. The party sued through a third-party complaint files an answer, similar to the one filed after the original complaint.

Notes for active learning

Discovery

A hallmark of the American legal system is the principle that there should be few surprises during a lawsuit. Since the late 1940s, the federal court system has required disclosing relevant facts and documents to the other side before trial, and virtually every state has followed this requirement. That disclosure is accomplished through a methodical process called *discovery*.

Discovery is the first phase in which the witness gets involved. Discovery takes three primary forms: written discovery (e.g., interrogatories) which must be answered under oath, document production, and depositions (i.e., sworn statements taken before a court officer). The parties exchange documents and other information about the litigation issues during discovery. The information is used in preparing the case for trial. Typically, third parties are involved in depositions, although there are provisions for written discovery and document requests to nonparties in many jurisdictions.

After discovery, the court typically reviews the facts of the case and determines if there is sufficient merit to proceed to trial or encourage the parties to settle. If the finding of facts determines the case to be frivolous or non-substantiated, the case is dismissed. If a substantial basis for the case is determined, the court will meet with and notify the parties of the trial schedule in the *pretrial order*.

Interrogatories and requests for admission

Interrogatories are questions requiring the opposing side's version of the facts and claims. They can be preprinted "form" interrogatories or specific questions asked. Questions can range from the broad ("What happened on Tuesday, June 18, 2021?") to the specific ("Is it your position that the defendant was wearing a blue jacket at 2:30 p.m. on May 13, 2021?"). If the questions asked are not fair or are difficult to understand, the party may object.

Requests for admission are not often used but can be a very powerful tool. They ask a party to admit or deny specific facts about the case, and they carry penalties for not answering, answering falsely, or answering late.

Document production

Each party has a right to see most documents arguably relate to a case. Particularly in more complex medical malpractice or product defect cases, the documents involved can be voluminous. Increasingly, courts are allowing access to computer files during document discovery. In cases where enough is at stake to justify it, courts have even allowed litigants to reconstruct deleted files (e.g., e-mail).

Depositions

Depositions are sworn statements when a person answers questions, and a court reporter makes a transcript of what is said. Depositions can range in length from an hour to weeks. Although attorneys have their strategies for depositions, there are three reasons to do them: to lock people into their stories, to see what the other side has, and to do a "practice trial," that is, to see how a witness will appear and conduct themselves before a judge or jury.

Depositions typically take place outside the courtroom, before a court recorder, with opposing counsel asking questions of the witness. The purpose of a deposition is to give facts, not speculate about what might have happened. Sometimes, "I don't know" is the correct answer. Second, it is human nature to want to explain things but resist the impulse. It is the opponent's responsibility to elicit the answers. The deponent should answer the question asked and not offer additional information.

Settlement avoids litigation

Most civil litigation cases never reach a final trial because a negotiated settlement is reached. Settlement ultimately means the plaintiff relinquishes their right to pursue the settled issue. For legal disputes, settlement can occur before or during litigation. Litigation is the dispute resolution process within the public court system after one party files a complaint and the other party answers. Settlement negotiation can be a formal or informal process. Parties can settle (i.e., agree) during informal negotiation or use a formal process called alternate dispute resolution (ADR), such as *mediation* or *arbitration*.

Some states and the federal system require litigants in civil actions to participate in alternative dispute resolution (ADR) in some form. The parties can agree to binding arbitration, and some contracts (insurance contracts and construction contracts, for example) require binding arbitration.

Often, the terms of the settlement are kept confidential. Sometimes, parties reach a settlement on specific issues in the case while a judge or jury needs to decide other issues. The Federal Rules of Evidence (and most state rules of evidence) provide that most settlement communications are inadmissible in court proceedings. Keeping these negotiations protected gives parties an incentive to have honest settlement discussions.

Typically, the court is either not involved or is involved informally. Judicial approval of civil settlements is usually required when one of the parties is a minor, a class action, or other circumstances that do not typically arise in most litigation.

Most criminal cases never go to trial either. Settlement may occur in criminal cases, though not in the same way as in civil cases. Sometimes, negotiations between the prosecution and defense lead to criminal charges being dismissed or a plea deal being reached. In criminal cases, the judge retains control over plea deals and can reject the agreement.

Motions to position the parties

In many cases, one or both parties try to have the dispute dismissed by motion. The parties present to the court those issues that are not in dispute, either because the parties agree or because the application of the law to the facts dictates a result.

The theory is that if a claim or lawsuit cannot possibly prevail, the parties and court should not waste time or money. Unfortunately, motion practice can be lengthy and expensive.

Summary judgment

In a trial, there are two overarching arguments. The attorneys argue about the law: determining which law applies and whether the law should be changed. Ultimately, questions of law are decided by the judge. The second argument is over the facts of each case, in other words, what happened. A jury usually decides the facts after considering testimony and other exhibits.

In many cases, the parties agree on some facts. When one party believes that there are no important facts in dispute, they file a motion for summary judgment. A typical summary judgment motion has three parts.

1) The facts: The plaintiff presents a version of the facts. The plaintiff usually attaches photos, signed statements from witnesses, and other evidence to support their statements.

2) The law: The plaintiff argues about the state of the law. The plaintiff's attorney prepares a memorandum that discusses the statutes and cases that govern the parties and attempt to convince the judge that, under the law, the plaintiff is entitled to win the case.

3) Even if…: In the last part of the summary judgment motion, the plaintiff anticipates what the defendant argues and tries to prove that the plaintiff will still win the case even if the defendant is correct in their arguments. For example, the plaintiff in a case about squatter's rights might claim they were living on a piece of property for 15 years but anticipates that the defendant will argue that the plaintiff has only been living on the property for 10 years. In this case, the plaintiff can argue that even if he had only been living on the property for 10 years, that is still enough time to win on a claim of squatter's rights.

The defendant responds. In their response, the defendant can show that the plaintiff's assertions about the law are incorrect, or evidence supports more than one version of the facts.

The judge's decision. After the papers and supporting evidence have been submitted, the judge reviews the paperwork and decides. The judge will grant the motion or agree with (in this example) the plaintiff if:

1) the plaintiff's arguments about the law were correct, and

2) even assuming the defendant's version of the facts was true, the plaintiff wins.

The judge will deny the motion if there is evidence that presents facts at trial.

Change of venue

Two basic requirements must be met before a court can hear a case.

1) *jurisdiction*, which means that the court can decide the legal issues affecting the parties' rights.

2) *venue*, which decides whether the court is in the best location to hear the case. Although this may sound unimportant, there are strict rules concerning where a case may be heard.

When one party wants to change venue, they must file a motion for change of venue. A motion for a change of venue ensures that a case is heard in the best location.

Most jurisdictions have strict requirements for the motion, which can be found in that jurisdiction's rules of procedure. Usually, a memorandum of law must accompany this motion, laying out the law and the arguments for why the venue should be moved. There are famous (or infamous) cases in a locality, and a party may wish to change venue so that jurors are less likely to have heard of the case and, therefore, be unbiased. Each state and federal jurisdiction has rules concerning venue

There are often rules about when a motion for change of venue may be filed during a case. If the venue is not challenged at the proper time, a challenge may be precluded.

Statutes of limitations

There are definite time limits to file a lawsuit. It depends upon the state (or federal law) and the offense. Some claims expire within a year after the event. Other claims can be filed decades later (e.g., tax fraud).

There are several ways that a statute of limitation may start, but the common three are:

1) The "date of harm." For example, the day you have a traffic accident will typically start the statute of limitations for suits regarding property damage to your car.

2) The date the harm was first discovered. The harm may lie dormant for a while and be discovered later. For example, hidden property damage until an inspection.

3) The date the harm should have been discovered. This is a less common standard, but in some instances, the period starts when the plaintiff should have discovered the harm, not when they did.

An exception is if the plaintiff sues a government agency. Because the government writes the rules, they have made it particularly difficult to sue them. In some instances, as little as 60 days to file a lawsuit is required to file an administrative complaint before filing a lawsuit.

There is much variation depending on the claim. Some statutes of limitations are:

- Libel or slander – 1 year

- Personal injury – 2 years

- Domestic violence – 3 years

- Medical malpractice – 3 years

- Breach of written contract – 4 years

- Breach of oral contract – 2 years

Notes for active learning

Trial Stage

The trial

If the parties do not reach an agreement or the dispute is not disposed of by motion, the case goes to trial. A trial is the plaintiff's opportunity to argue their case for obtaining a judgment against the defendant. A trial represents the defendant's chance to refute the plaintiff's case and offer evidence related to the dispute. In a civil trial, a judge or jury examines the evidence to decide whether, by a "preponderance of the evidence," the defendant should be held legally responsible for the damages alleged by the plaintiff.

Although a trial is the most high-profile phase of a civil lawsuit, most civil disputes are resolved before trial (or before a lawsuit is filed) via settlement between the parties. This process can include alternative dispute resolution (ADR) like arbitration or dismissal of the case.

The following six main phases of a civil trial is presented in the context of a typical "plaintiff *v.* defendant civil case.

1) Jury selection

2) Opening statements

3) Witness testimony and cross-examination

4) Closing arguments

5) Jury instructions

6) Jury deliberation and verdict

At trial, the attorneys (or the parties, if they are not represented) present evidence and legal arguments, and the judge (or jury) decides the facts. The trial is the other point at which third parties can become involved. The attorney for the party who wants a person to testify may subpoena them for trial. Witnesses can be called to testify at any time, from shortly after the event to almost a decade after.

After both sides present their arguments, the judge or jury considers whether to find the defendant liable for the plaintiff's claimed damages, and if so, to what extent (i.e., the amount of money damages a defendant must pay, or fashion another remedy).

Depending on the type of case, a civil trial may not necessarily focus only on the plaintiff's allegations and the defendant's liability. For example, in most divorce cases, a trial judge decides after hearing allegations from both sides of the dispute and enters a judgment that may favor one spouse on one issue (e.g., child custody) and the other spouse as to another issue (e.g., alimony). Once the judge or jury has reached a decision, the judge orders judgment. The judge may order that one party pay the attorney's fees, although such awards are unusual.

Either party may appeal a judge's decision to a higher court. However, it is unusual for an appeals court to overturn a judge's decision. Settlements usually cannot be appealed if both parties agree to their terms. The process can take from six months to years. Generally, the less money in dispute and the more issues are resolved before trial, the faster the lawsuit.

Jury selection

In most civil cases, either party can choose to have a jury. Whether to request a jury is extremely important. Except in cases that are tried before a judge (e.g., family court cases), an initial step in a civil trial is selecting a jury.

During jury selection, the judge (and usually the attorneys) questions a pool of potential jurors regarding general matters or about knowledge or preformed opinions about the case – this process is *voire dire*. These questions probe personal ideological predispositions or life experiences that pertain to the case. The judge can excuse potential jurors at this stage based on their responses.

Either the plaintiff or defendant may exclude a certain number of jurors by using peremptory challenges and challenges for cause.

A *peremptory challenge* excludes a juror for any reason.

A *challenge for cause* excludes a juror who cannot be objective in deciding the case.

Opening statements

Once a jury is selected, the first "dialogue" in a personal injury trial comes in the form of two opening statements -- one from the plaintiff's attorney and the other from an attorney representing the defendant.

Statements to the jury made first by the plaintiffs' attorney and then by the defense attorneys setting up the circumstances and rationale of the legal complaint (plaintiffs) and the reasons for dismissing the claim (defense). No witnesses testify at this stage, and no physical evidence is ordinarily utilized.

Because the plaintiff must demonstrate the defendant's legal liability based on the plaintiff's allegations, the plaintiff's opening statement is usually given first. It is often more detailed than that of the defendant. In some cases, the defendant may wait until the plaintiff's main case concludes before making its opening statement.

Regardless of when opening statements are made in a personal injury case, during those statements:

- The plaintiff presents the facts of the case and the defendant's alleged role in causing the plaintiff's damages (or reasons to find for the plaintiff) -- walking the jury through what the plaintiff intends to demonstrate to get a civil judgment against the defendant.

- The defendant's attorney gives the jury the defense's interpretation of the facts and sets the stage for rebutting the plaintiff's key evidence and presenting any "affirmative" defenses to the plaintiff's allegations (or reasons to find for the defendant).

When a civil lawsuit involves multiple parties (i.e., three individual plaintiffs sue one defendant, or one plaintiff sues two separate defendants), attorneys representing each party may give distinct opening arguments.

Evidence and arguments

Plaintiff testimony

At the heart of any civil trial is often called the "case-in-chief," the stage at which each side presents its key evidence and arguments to the jury. In its case-in-chief, the plaintiff methodically sets forth its evidence to convince the jury that the defendant is legally responsible for the plaintiff's damages or that judgment for the plaintiff is warranted under the circumstances.

At this point, the plaintiff may call witnesses and experts to testify to strengthen their case. The plaintiff may introduce physical evidence, such as photographs, documents, and medical reports.

In complicated civil lawsuits (e.g., employment discrimination, defective product claims), plaintiffs use expert testimony and documentary evidence as crucial in proving the defendant's legal liability. Documents must be authentic. There are many evidence rules to ensure that the item in evidence is the actual evidence, or at least an accurate copy. The rules of evidence govern what may and may not be considered when the jury decides the outcome of a case.

Defense testimony

After the plaintiff concludes its case-in-chief and "rests," the defendant can present its evidence in the same proactive manner, seeking to show that it is not liable for the plaintiff's claimed harm. The defense may call its witnesses to the stand and present independent evidence to refute or downplay the key elements of the plaintiff's allegations.

Once the defense has rested, the plaintiff has an opportunity to respond to the defense's arguments through a process known as "rebuttal," a brief period during which the plaintiff may only contradict the defense's evidence (rather than present new arguments). Sometimes, the defense may, in turn, have a chance to respond to the prosecution's rebuttal.

Once the plaintiff and defendant each present their case and challenge the evidence presented by the other, both sides "rest," meaning that no more evidence will be presented to the jury before closing arguments are made.

Witness testimony and cross-examination

Whether called by the plaintiff or defendant, witness testimony usually adheres to the following formula:

- The witness is called to the stand and is "sworn in," taking an oath *to tell the truth.*

- The party who called the witness to the stand questions the witness through "direct" examination, eliciting information through question-and-answer to strengthen the party's position in the dispute.

- After direct examination, the opposing party has an opportunity to question the witness through "cross-examination." Cross-examination tries to discredit the witness's story, credibility, or otherwise discredit the witness and their testimony.

- After cross-examination, the side that originally called the witness has a second opportunity to question him or her through "re-direct examination" and attempt to remedy any damaging effects of cross-examination.

Witnesses may only present facts that they observed. A witness can say, "I saw the blue car drive through a red light before hitting the pedestrian," but a witness cannot say something like, "The driver of the blue car should go to jail because he ran a red light and hurt someone," because it is the witness's opinion that the driver should go to jail. Lawyers are not allowed to ask leading questions, such as "Where did the blue car go through the red light?" because it suggests to the witness that this event occurred.

Every witness must be able to be cross-examined. Cross-examination is the part of the trial when one attorney tries to discover untruths or other issues with a witness's testimony. The right to cross-examine stems from the 6th Amendment right of the accused to confront the accuser. It ensures that all testimony is rigorously examined before going to a jury. "Hearsay testimony" are statements about what another told the witness and are generally not allowed when the original person is not in court. However, there are exceptions to this rule.

At the discretion of the judge, each witness can be redirected after cross-examination by either counsel. If critical information is not divulged during the initial testimony, counsel can request to *recall* a witness to the stand for additional questioning and cross-examination.

Judges rule on objections

When a lawyer says "objection" during court, they tell the judge that they think their opponent violated a rule of procedure. The judge's ruling determines what the jury is allowed to consider when deciding the verdict of a case.

A judge can either "overrule" the objection or "sustain" it. When an objection is overruled, it means that the evidence is properly admitted to the court, and the trial can proceed.

When an objection is sustained, the lawyer must rephrase the question or otherwise address the issue with the evidence to ensure that the jury only hears properly admitted evidence. In theory, the jury should disregard the improper question asked, although this can be difficult to do.

An objection is essential to procedure even if it is overruled. Once a lawyer objects to some evidence, that objection is on the record. If the lawyer disagrees with the judge's ruling, they can appeal that decision. If the lawyer failed to object to evidence, they lose the right to appeal, even if the evidence was admitted improperly.

Closing arguments

Like the opening statement, the closing argument offers the plaintiff and the defendant in a civil dispute a chance to "sum up" the case, recapping the evidence in a light favorable to their respective positions. This is the final chance for the parties to address the jury before deliberations.

In closing arguments, the plaintiff seeks to show why the evidence requires the jury to find the defendant legally responsible for the plaintiff's damages or why the plaintiff's case is stronger than the defendants. The defendant tries to show that the plaintiff has fallen short of establishing the defendant's liability for any civil judgment in the plaintiff's favor.

Closing arguments are typically intended to be dramatic and pointed for effect.

Jury instruction

After both sides have presented their arguments and evidence, the judge (in a bench trial) or jury (jury trial) considers whether to find the defendant liable for the plaintiff's damages, and if so, to what extent (i.e., the amount of money damages a defendant must pay, or some other remedy).

Jury instructions are the process in which the judge gives the jury the set of legal standards needed to decide whether the defendant should be held accountable for the plaintiff's alleged harm.

The judge decides what legal standards apply to the defendant's case based on the issues and evidence presented during the trial. Often, this process has input from the plaintiff and defendant. The judge instructs the jury on relevant legal principles, including findings the jury must make to arrive at certain conclusions. The judge describes critical legal concepts (e.g., "preponderance of the evidence"), defines claims the jury may consider (i.e., *fraud, breach of contract, emotional distress*); and discusses types of damages (i.e., compensatory, and punitive) based on the evidence presented at trial.

After the judge provides the jury with specific oral instructions regarding its evaluation of the case, the jury is dismissed to deliberate, in private, the outcome of the case.

Jury deliberation, verdict and judgment

After receiving instruction from the judge, the jurors as a group consider the case through a process of "deliberation" and attempt to agree on whether the defendant should be held liable based on the plaintiff's claims. If so, the appropriate compensation for any damages. Deliberation is the first opportunity for the jury to discuss the case. Deliberations are a methodical process lasting from a few hours to several weeks.

Once the jury reaches a decision (may take hours to days), the jury foreperson informs the judge, and the judge announces the verdict in open court.

Most states require that a 12-person jury in a personal injury case be unanimous in finding for the plaintiff or the defendant, though some states allow for verdicts based on a majority as low as 9 to 3.

If the jury fails to reach a unanimous (or sufficient majority) verdict and is at a standstill (i.e., a *hung* jury), the judge may declare a *mistrial*; the case may be dismissed, or a trial starts again with jury selection.

Following the rendering of the verdict, the court can rule and concur requesting final judgment or determine if a new trial is required or if the case should be dismissed.

Post-Trial Stage

Appealing a court decision

Most civil and criminal decisions of a state or federal trial court (and administrative decisions by agencies) are subject to review by an appeals court. Whether the appeal concerns a judge's order or a jury's verdict, an appeals court reviews what happened in prior proceedings for any errors of law or procedure. The losing party cannot appeal a case just because they are unhappy with the outcome; they may only challenge decisions that may have resulted from errors, such as a misinterpretation of legal precedent or reliance on evidence that should have been excluded and not presented to the jury.

If the court finds an error contributing to the trial court's decision, the appeals court will reverse that decision. The parties submit briefs to the court and may be granted an oral argument before the panel of judges. Once an appeals court has made its decision, the opportunity for further appeals is limited. As the number of parties filing appeals has risen substantially, the state and federal court systems have implemented changes to manage the appeals process.

Trials *vs.* appeals

A trial and an appeal have a few similarities but many significant differences. The parties present their cases at trial, call witnesses for testimony, and present evidence (e.g., documents, photographs, reports, surveys, diaries). The jury evaluates the veracity of the evidence and determines the facts of the case; what they believe happened. A jury is sometimes referred to as the "finder of fact."

The judge controls the activities in the courtroom and makes the legal decisions, such as ruling on motions and objections raised by the attorneys. The judge is often called the "finder of law." If the parties have chosen a bench trial rather than a jury trial, the judge makes both fact and law findings.

Appeals overview

An appeal is a review of the trial court's application of the law. There is no jury in an appeal, nor do the lawyers present witnesses or other evidence. The court accepts the facts as revealed in the trial court unless a factual finding is clearly against the weight of the evidence.

Another difference between a trial and an appeal is the number of judges involved. A single judge presides over a trial while several judges hear an appeal, depending on the jurisdiction. At the initial appeals court level, courts may have three to a few dozen (en banc) judges.

However, the total number of judges seldom hear claims together. Instead, appeals are typically heard by panels, often comprised of three judges. In rare instances, the full court may decide to grant a motion for rehearing *en banc* when all the judges on the appeals court hear the case and issue a decision. At the state and federal level, Supreme Courts have from five to nine justices (i.e., justices are judges on the highest appeals court in the jurisdiction).

Appellate briefs

The main form of persuasion on appeal is the written appellate brief, filed by counsel for each party. With this brief, the party that lost in the trial court argues that the trial judge incorrectly applied the law. The party that won below will argue that the trial court's decision was correct. Both parties support their positions concerning applicable case law and statutes.

An appeal is a more scholarly proceeding than a trial. Whereas the litigator must be an active strategist in the courtroom, calling witnesses, cross-examining, and making motions or objections, the appellate lawyer builds their case in the brief before the appeal is heard. Appeals often include a short period for oral argument, but the judges often consume this period with questions for the attorney, prompted by the briefs.

The "record" on appeal

Appeals court decisions turn on the record, which documents what happened in the trial court. The record contains the pleadings (i.e., plaintiff's complaint and defendant's answer), pretrial motions, a transcript of what occurred during the trial, the exhibits put into evidence, post-trial motions, and any discussion with the judge that did not take place "off the record." The success of an appeal, therefore, depends on what occurred at trial. If an attorney fails to get critical, available evidence into the record or object to something prejudicial, the opportunity to do so is lost.

Post appeal

The party that loses in a state or federal appeals court may appeal to the state supreme court or the U.S. Supreme Court. Most states call their highest court *Supreme Court*, though Maryland and New York call theirs the *Court of Appeals*.

Review in appeals courts, however, is discretionary. Because the U.S. Supreme Court receives many more requests for review than practical, they typically grant review only to cases involving unsettled questions of law (e.g., different decisions within the federal circuit courts). The U.S. Supreme Court can only review cases that raise federal or constitutional issues. Cases concerning state law exclusively are beyond Supreme Court jurisdiction. At the highest appellate court, the parties have litigated and had the case reviewed at least once, reducing decisions that are biased or contrary to law.

Notes for active learning

Civil Litigation Timeline

Able v. Baker

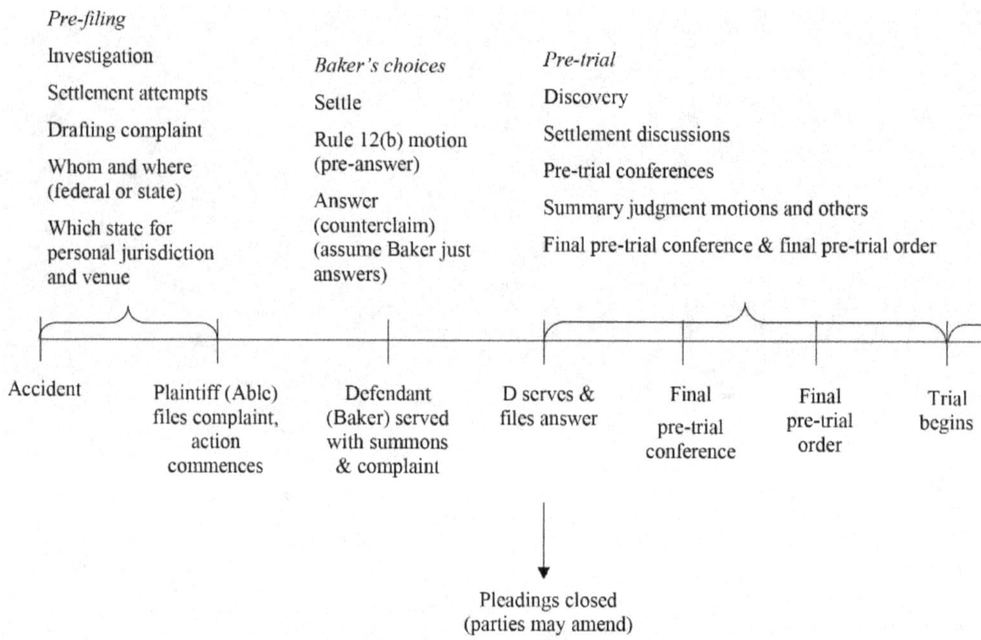

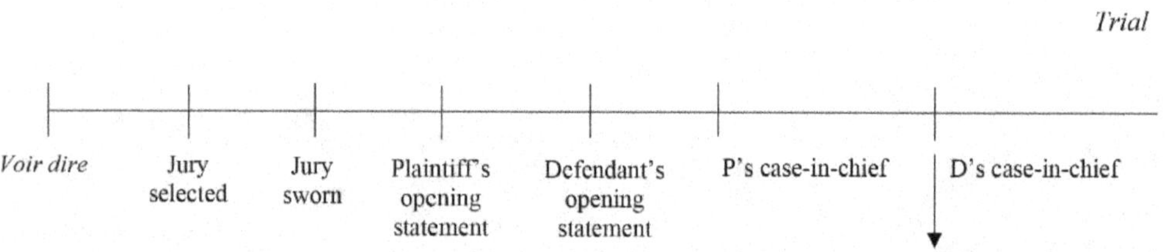

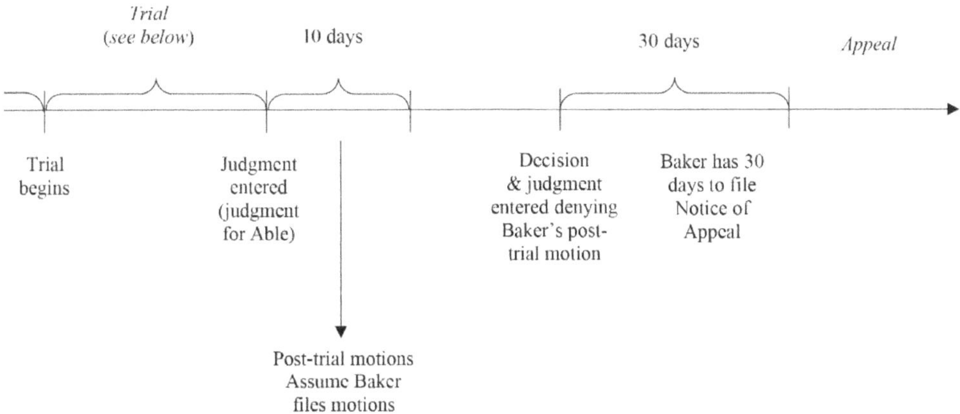

Trial
(see below)
10 days
30 days
Appeal
Trial
begins
Judgment
entered
(judgment
for Able)
Decision
& judgment
entered denying
Baker's post-
trial motion
Baker has 30
days to file
Notice of
Appeal
Post-trial motions
Assume Baker
files motions

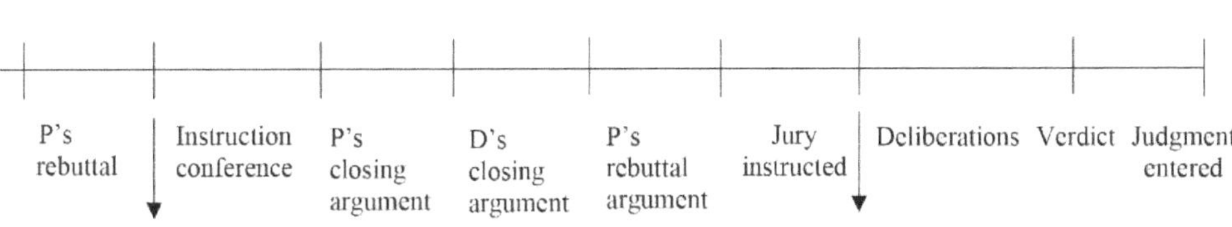

P's
rebuttal
Instruction
conference
P's
closing
argument
D's
closing
argument
P's
rebuttal
argument
Jury
instructed
Deliberations
Verdict
Judgment
entered

Notes for active learning

Subpoenas

A *subpoena* [Latin, *under penalty*] is a court-ordered command to produce documents or appear for a proceeding.

The subpoena requires a person to *do* something (e.g., testify, present information) as facts in a pending case.

A *subpoena ad testificandum* requires a person to testify before a court or other legal authority.

A *subpoena duces tecum* requires a person to produce documents, materials, or tangible evidence.

A subpoena may be requested in any matter, but common issues involve divorce, child custody, and personal injury.

Purpose of a subpoena

Under state and federal civil procedure, subpoenas offer parties a chance to obtain information to prove their case.

Criminal attorneys use subpoenas to obtain *witness* or *lay opinion* (i.e., personal experience) testimony from a third party to support the defendant's innocence.

Civil attorneys subpoena individuals and businesses for information that may help settle a claim.

For example, an attorney representing a spouse in a child custody hearing might issue a subpoena to the other spouse to appear in court to determine joint custody arrangements.

Examples of subpoenas include requests for computer files and downloaded material, income tax returns, photographs, graphs, & charts, blood test results, DNA samples, medical, insurance, and employee records.

Authority to issue subpoenas

A subpoena is typically requested by an attorney and issued by a court clerk, magistrate, or judge.

For specific purposes, a subpoena may be issued and signed by an attorney on behalf of the court in which the attorney is authorized to practice law.

If the subpoena is for a high-level government official (e.g., governor, agency head), it must be signed by an administrative law judge.

In some cases, a non-lawyer may issue a subpoena if acting on their behalf (*pro se* litigant).

Serving a subpoena

Depending on the jurisdiction, a subpoena may be served as follows:

> Hand-delivered (known as "personal delivery" method);

> E-mailed to the last known e-mail address of the individual (receipt acknowledgment requested);

> Certified mail to the last known address (return receipt requested); or

> Hearing it read aloud.

Responding to a subpoena

A subpoena is part of a court's legal process, and failure to respond is considered *contempt of court*.

The subpoena specifies what is requested or who is to appear.

Subpoena requests for documents are detailed, allowing adequate preparation for testimony at trial or proceeding.

Penalties for failure to comply

A subpoena is a court-ordered command. A person who receives a subpoena but does not comply with its terms may be subject to civil or criminal contempt of court charges and penalties (e.g., fines, jail time, or both).

Civil contempt occurs when a person fails to produce documents requested or fails to obey the terms of a subpoena and, thereby, hinders the judicial process.

Penalties for contempt of court include fines, imprisonment, or both.

Contempt charges apply until the party agrees to produce the requested information and perform legal obligations.

Criminal contempt, usually intended as punishment, refers to disruptive conduct or disrespectful behavior at court.

Criminal contempt includes the refusal to submit documents or other data.

Refusing to produce documents

Defenses for failure to produce documents or appear in court may include claims that the information sought is privileged, lost, violates a person's Fifth Amendment right against self-incrimination, or the requests are overbroad or unduly burdensome.

Alternative Dispute Resolution (ADR)

Alternative dispute resolution (ADR) advantages and disadvantages

Using the court system to resolve disputes can take years and cost thousands, if not millions, for legal fees and expenses. Parties increasingly use alternative dispute resolution (ADR) methods to resolve disputes. The advantages of ADR, as compared to traditional litigation, are the efficiency of costs and time. ADR saves much money, in large part because it saves much time. In commercial litigation, the ordinary business operations of the parties are often disrupted. Moreover, because ADR is faster and less expensive than traditional litigation, it is much less stressful for the participants, which is another advantage.

There are some disadvantages of ADR, however. The process has been criticized as a waste of time by some legal commentators who believe that the same time could be spent pursuing civil court claims. ADR prevents the parties from getting their day in court, and for some litigants, this is a reason to use adversarial litigation. Arbitration awards, for instance, are challenging to overturn on appeal.

Types of ADR

Several processes qualify as *alternative dispute resolution* (ADR). Parties may agree that a negotiated settlement is preferred to investing time and money in protracted civil litigation.

Common forms of ADR include negotiation, mediation, arbitration, conciliation, minitrials, and fact-finding.

Many ADR techniques have little in common except that negotiation is prominent. Mediation and arbitration and are frequently used alternative dispute resolution techniques.

Negotiation

Negotiation plays a vital role in each method, either primarily or secondarily. For example, it is not uncommon for parties to begin negotiations with early neutral evaluation and then move to nonbinding mediation. If mediation fails, the parties may proceed with binding arbitration. The goal with each type of ADR is for the parties to find the most effective way of resolving their dispute without litigation. Many participants in unsuccessful ADR proceedings believe it is helpful to determine that their disputes are not amenable to a negotiated settlement before commencing a lawsuit.

Conciliation

Conciliation focuses on the early stages of negotiation, such as opening communication channels, bringing the disputants together, and identifying points of mutual agreement. Mediation focuses on the later stages of negotiation, exploring weaknesses in each party's position, investigating areas where the parties disagree but might be inclined to compromise, and suggesting mutually agreeable outcomes.

Mediation

Mediation consists of assisted negotiations where the disputants agree to enlist a neutral intermediary. The mediator facilitates a voluntary, mutually acceptable settlement. Their primary function is to identify issues, explore agreements, discuss the consequences of an impasse, and encourage considering the other party's interests. However, unlike arbitrators, mediators lack the power to impose a decision on the parties.

Mediation is referred to as conciliation or conciliated negotiation. However, the terms are not necessarily interchangeable. Conciliation and mediation typically work well when the disputants are involved in a long-term relationship (e.g., married partners, wholesalers, retailers) and intricate problems not easily solved by all-or-nothing solutions (e.g., antitrust suits with many complex issues).

Although some jurisdictions have enacted statutes governing mediation, most mediation proceedings are voluntary. Accordingly, a mediator's influence is limited by the autonomy of the parties and their willingness to negotiate in good faith. Thus, a mediator can go no further than the parties are willing to go.

Since agreements reached by mediation bear the parties' imprint, many observers feel more likely to adhere to decisions imposed than arbitration or court mandates. Disputants who participate in mediation without legal representation are likely to adhere to settlements when the alternative is civil litigation. Attorneys' fees consume a significant portion of any monetary award granted to the parties.

Arbitration

Arbitration refers the dispute to an impartial intermediary chosen by the parties who agree to abide by the arbitrator's award issued after a hearing where the parties have the opportunity to be heard. Arbitration resembles traditional civil litigation in that a neutral intermediary hears arguments and imposes a final and binding decision.

In arbitration, the parties elect to settle future disputes without judicial intervention. The disputants select the intermediary who serves as an arbitrator. Arbitration resembles litigation as parties use arbitration for facilitated settlement negotiations. Parties using arbitration often fail to commence serious negotiations until the arbitration proceedings begin.

In civil litigation, the judicial system is generally chosen by an aggrieved party after a dispute has materialized. Thus, parties to civil litigation have little to no control over who presided in the judicial proceedings.

Frequently, negotiations continue with the arbitration proceedings, the parties' representatives discuss settlement as hearings are underway. Arbitration expedites negotiations since the parties know that the decision is typically final and rarely appealable once the arbitrator issues a decision.

Private arbitration

Private contractual arbitration agreements are used by parties where disputes arise and prefer alternative dispute resolutions compared to a judicial remedy. The arbitrator need not be a judge or government official. Instead, an effective arbitrator is a person whom the parties feel has knowledge, experience, and objectivity to resolve the dispute. In some states, legislation prescribes the qualifications to be an arbitrator.

An arbitrator's power is derived from the arbitration agreement, limiting issues that the arbitrator has the authority to resolve. In many states, arbitration agreements are supported by statutes providing judicial enforcement of agreements and respecting arbitrator-rendered awards.

Statutes governing private arbitration often set forth criteria that must be followed before an arbitration agreement is binding and enforceable by a court. A court typically deems the arbitrator's decision final, and the losing party may only appeal the decision upon a showing of fraud, misrepresentation, or arbitrariness by the arbitrator.

Private arbitration is the primary method of settling labor disputes between unions and employers. For example, unions and employers include a collective bargaining arbitration agreements clause in contracts. The union and employer agree to arbitrate future employee grievances (e.g., wages, hours, working conditions, job security). Many real estate and insurance contracts specify arbitration as the exclusive resolution method for disputes between the parties entering into these types of relationships.

Judicial arbitration

Judicial arbitration is a non-binding form of arbitration. Judicial arbitration is usually mandated by statute or court rules that govern disputes exceeding the jurisdiction of small claims court but insufficient for trial in civil court. A party dissatisfied with the arbitrator's decision may proceed to trial rather than accept the decision. Most jurisdictions prescribe a specific period within which the parties to a judicial arbitration may reject the arbitrator's decision and litigate. If this period expires before either party rejects the arbitrator's decision, the decision becomes final, binding, and judicially enforceable, like a private arbitrator's decision.

Non-binding judicial arbitration in federal court

Several federal district courts also have mandatory programs for non-binding judicial arbitration funded by Congress. For example, the Local Rules of Court may require non-binding arbitration for disputes not expected to exceed $200,000. Since judicial arbitration is mandatory but non-binding, it facilitates settlement negotiations. Arbitration reduces civil court calendars that may have hundreds of lawsuits to improve judicial efficiency.

The policy is that by mandating nonbinding arbitration, the parties value a negotiated settlement. Seldom do litigants receive everything demanded in their petitions or complaints. Private and judicial arbitration is generally less costly and more time-efficient than formal civil litigation. The typical arbitration takes 4 to 5 months, while litigation may take years. The cost of arbitration is minimal compared to civil trials since the American Arbitration Association charges a nominal filing fee. The arbitrator may work without a fee to broaden their professional experience.

Minitrials

A minitrial is a process by which the attorneys present a brief version of the case to a panel, often comprised of the clients and a neutral intermediary who chairs the process. Expert witnesses (or lay witnesses) present the case. After the presentation, the clients, typically top management representatives, attempt to negotiate a settlement. If a negotiated settlement is not reached, the parties may allow the intermediary to mediate the dispute or render a non-binding advisory opinion regarding the likely outcome if tried in civil court.

Businesses use minitrials to resolve large-scale disputes involving product liability, antitrust issues, billion-dollar construction contracts, and mass tort or disaster litigation. Minitrials are effective because they bring top management together to negotiate the legal issues underlying a dispute. Early in the negotiation process, upper management is sometimes preoccupied with the business side of a dispute. Minitrials shift management's focus to outstanding legal issues. Minitrials allow businesses a forum for face-to-face negotiations. Management also generally prefers the time-saving, abbreviated nature of minitrials over time-consuming and costly civil litigation. Minitrials expedite negotiations by making them more realistic. Once the parties have seen their case play out in court, they are less likely to posture over less relevant or meaningless issues.

Summary jury trials

Summary jury trials are used primarily in federal courts. They allow parties to *litigate* their cases before an advisory panel of jurors without a final decision as rendered by a jury in civil court. The purpose of the summary jury trial is to facilitate pretrial settlement. A significant impediment to negotiation is a disagreement between the parties (and their attorneys) regarding a civil jury's likely findings on liability or damages. Like minitrials, summary jury trials give the parties a chance to reach a preliminary assessment of the strengths and weaknesses and proceed with negotiations after the advisory jury's findings.

Summary jury trials and minitrials can be scheduled and completed before formal civil cases usually reach the court docket. Summary jury trials are presided over by a judge or magistrate in a federal district court. Evidentiary and procedural rules are few and flexible. For example, a ten-member jury venire is presented to counsel. Counsel is provided with a short juror character profile and given two challenges to select a final six-member jury for the proceeding. Each attorney has one hour to argue their case to the jury.

After counsel's presentations, the presiding official delivers a brief statement of the applicable law to the jury, and the jury retires to deliberate. Juries are encouraged to return a consensus verdict but may return a special report that anonymously lists each juror's view regarding liability and damages. After the verdict or special report has been returned, counsel meets with the adjudicating official to discuss the verdict and establish a timetable for settlement negotiations.

Early neutral evaluation

Early neutral evaluation is an informal process by which a neutral intermediary is appointed to hear facts and arguments by the parties. In some jurisdictions, early neutral evaluation is a court-ordered alternative dispute resolution technique, the option of hiring a neutral intermediary or having the court appoint one.

After the hearing, the intermediary evaluates the parties' strengths and weaknesses and potential exposure to liability for money damages. The parties, counsel, and intermediary then engage in discussions designed to assist the parties in identifying the agreed-upon facts, isolating the issues in dispute, locating areas in which further investigation would be helpful, and devising a plan streamlining the investigative process. Settlement negotiations and mediation may follow, but only if the parties desire.

The objective of an early neutral evaluation is to obtain an initial assessment of the dispute by an objective intermediary with sufficient knowledge and experience to sift through the facts and issues and find the ground shared by the parties and the ground separating them. Much like in the other forms of alternative dispute resolution, the success of early neutral evaluation depends mainly on the party's credence in the process. It also depends in large part on the disputants' willingness to compromise and settle the dispute. Nevertheless, successful early neutral evaluations can lead directly to meaningful negotiations.

Alternative dispute resolution and civil litigation

The procedures and techniques discussed are the most common methods of ADR. However, despite its success over the past three decades, ADR is not the appropriate choice for all legal disputes. Many individuals and entities still resist ADR because it lacks the substantive, procedural, and evidentiary protections of formal civil litigation.

For example, parties to ADR typically waive their rights to object to evidence that might be deemed inadmissible under the court's rules. Hearsay evidence is a typical example of evidence that the parties and intermediaries consider in ADR forums but is generally excluded from civil trials. For example, suppose a disputant believes that they would be sacrificing too many rights and protections by waiving civil litigation formalities. In that case, ADR will not be the appropriate method of dispute resolution.

Exhibit 1: Complaint

UNITED STATES DISTRICT COURT FOR THE
EASTERN DISTRICT OF VIRGINIA

Civil Action No. 20-CV-1234

John Able,	)	
Plaintiff	)	COMPLAINT
v.	)	
Joseph Baker,	)	
Defendant	)	

1. Jurisdiction is founded on 28 U.S.C. § 1332. Plaintiff is a citizen of the state of Virginia. Defendant is a citizen of the state of Maryland. The amount in controversy exceeds $75,000, exclusive of interest and costs.

2. On January 12, 1999, the plaintiff was driving east on Virginia Beach Boulevard in Virginia Beach, Virginia. Plaintiff entered the intersection of Virginia Beach Boulevard and Witchduck Road when the traffic light directing eastbound Virginia Beach Boulevard traffic through the intersection was green.

3. While the plaintiff's car was in the intersection, the defendant, driving north on Witchduck Road, negligently drove his car into the intersection and the plaintiff's automobile.

4. As a result of the defendant's negligence, the plaintiff suffered physical injuries, including broken bones, muscle, ligament, tendon damage, bruises, and cuts. Plaintiff also suffered pain and emotional distress. Plaintiff required treatment at a hospital and was forced to be absent for two weeks from his job. Plaintiff also incurred expenses for physical therapy and continuing medical treatment.

Wherefore, the plaintiff demands judgment against the defendant for $650,000 plus costs and any other relief the court deems just in the circumstances.

Dated: July 25, 2020

                                Gordon Smith
                                Jones, Smith & Black
                                123 Granby Street
                                Norfolk, VA
                                (100) 100-1111
                                Attorneys for Plaintiff

Exhibit 2: Summons

UNITED STATES DISTRICT COURT FOR THE
EASTERN DISTRICT OF VIRGINIA

Civil Action No. 20-CV-1234

John Able,	)	
Plaintiff	)	SUMMONS
v.	)	
Joseph Baker,	)	
Defendant	)	

To the above named Defendant:

You are hereby summoned and required to serve upon Gordon Howe, 123 Granby Street, Norfolk, Virginia, plaintiff's attorney, an answer to the complaint served upon you with this summons, within 20 days after service of this summons upon you, exclusive of the day of service. If you fail to answer by that time, judgment by default will be taken against you for the relief demanded in the complaint.

[s]________________________________

Clerk of Court

[Seal of the U.S. District Court for the

Eastern District of Virginia]

Dated: July 25, 2020

Exhibit 3: Answer

UNITED STATES DISTRICT COURT FOR THE

EASTERN DISTRICT OF VIRGINIA

Civil Action No. 20-CV-1234

John Able,	)	
Plaintiff	)	ANSWER
v.	)	
Joseph Baker,	)	
Defendant	)	

1. Defendant admits the allegations in paragraph 1 of the plaintiff's complaint.

2. Defendant admits that plaintiff was driving east on Virginia Beach Boulevard. Defendant has insufficient information to admit or deny the other allegations in paragraph 2.

3. Defendant denies the allegations in paragraph 3.

4. Defendant denies that plaintiff suffered injury as a result of any negligence by the defendant. Defendant has insufficient information to admit or deny the remaining allegations in paragraph 4.

Wherefore, defendant asks that plaintiff take nothing by this action, plus any other relief the court deems.

Dated: September 3, 2020

Austin Powers

Powers & Evil

321 Granby Street

Norfolk, VA

(100) 000-0000

Attorneys for Defendant

Exhibit 4: Judgment in a civil case

UNITED STATES DISTRICT COURT FOR THE

EASTERN DISTRICT OF VIRGINIA

Civil Action No. 20-CV-1234

John Able,	)	
Plaintiff	)	JUDGMENT IN A CIVIL CASE
v.	)	
Joseph Baker,	)	
Defendant	)	

Judgment is to be entered as follows:

Upon the jury's verdict, plaintiff John Able is awarded $200,000 damages from defendant, Joseph Baker, plus costs.

Dated: February 8, 2021

[s] _______________________________

Clerk of Court

Exhibit 5: Notice of appeal

UNITED STATES DISTRICT COURT FOR THE

EASTERN DISTRICT OF VIRGINIA

Civil Action No. 20-CV-1234

John Able,	)	
Plaintiff	)	NOTICE OF APPEAL
v.	)	
Joseph Baker,	)	
Defendant	)	

Defendant gives notice that he is appealing the court's judgment entered February 8, 2000.

Dated: February 28, 2021

Austin Powers

Powers & Evil

321 Granby Street

Norfolk, VA

(100) 000-0000

Attorneys for Defendant

Exhibit 6: Docket

UNITED STATES DISTRICT COURT FOR THE

EASTERN DISTRICT OF VIRGINIA

Civil Action No. 20-CV-1234

John Able,	)
Plaintiff	)
v.	)
Joseph Baker,	)
Defendant	)

DOCKET

7/25/20 – Plaintiff files Complaint; Summons issues.

8/23/20 – Return of Summons, Defendant served summons and complaint.

9/3/20 – Defendant files Answer.

    [Omissions up to judgment]

2/8/21 – Enter Judgment: Upon the jury's verdict, plaintiff John Able is awarded $300,000 damages from defendant, Joseph Baker, plus costs.

2/28/21 – Defendant files Notice of appeal.

Appendix

Overview of American Law

History of American law

As the American colonies were settled, they relied on the English legal system, known as *common law*.

Principles announced in case decisions are precedent (i.e., guidance) for judges deciding similar disputes.

Three separate courts were established to resolve disputes:

1) Law courts

   Before 1066, the local lord was in charge of the locality and resolved disputes as he saw fit.

   After the Norman Conquest (1066), these localized courts were replaced with a uniform law system.

   Followers of William the Conqueror were appointed to administer justice uniformly in courts of law.

   The focus was on procedure rather than the merits of the case.

   Damages were in the form of monetary relief or compensation.

2) Chancery (equity) courts

   Addressed situations where the result in the law court was unfair or could not be corrected by monetary awards (e.g., injunction).

   Equity courts focus on the merits of the case rather than strict adherence to procedure.

   Remedies are shaped to fit each dispute.

3) Merchant courts for trade disputes

   Rules were developed by the merchants who traveled throughout Europe to resolve disputes that uniformly arose from trade.

   Rules evolved to the law of merchants based upon common trade practice and usage.

   Eventually, separate merchant courts adjudicated trade disputes.

Adoption of English common law in America

Except for Louisiana, states base their legal systems primarily on English common law.

The law, equity, and merchant courts have been merged.

Most U.S. courts permit the aggrieved party to seek both law (i.e., money damages) and equitable remedies (i.e., injunctions, declaratory judgments).

Civil codes and statutory laws

The civil law system models the Romano-Germanic codified legal system.

Civil code and parliamentary statutes proclaim and interpret the law as the sole sources of the law.

The adjudication of a case is applying the code or statutes to a specific set of facts.

In some civil law countries, court decisions do not have the force of law unless codified into law.

Functions of the law

Although a precise definition of law is complex, it is generally agreed that law must be obeyed and followed, and disobedience is subject to penalty.

The law is often described by the function it serves within a society. The primary functions served by the law in this country are to:

1) keep the peace, which includes making certain activities crimes;

2) shape moral standards, which includes prohibiting certain activities that society considers inappropriate or wrong;

3) promote social justice, such as enacting laws that prohibit wrongful discrimination;

4) maintain the status quo, which includes passing laws preventing the forceful overthrow of the government;

5) facilitate orderly change, such as passing statutes after public debate and input;

6) facilitate planning, commercial laws allowing businesses to plan and allocate resources;

7) provide a basis for compromise since 90 percent of lawsuits are settled prior to trial; and

8) maximize individual freedom, evidenced by the Bill of Rights.

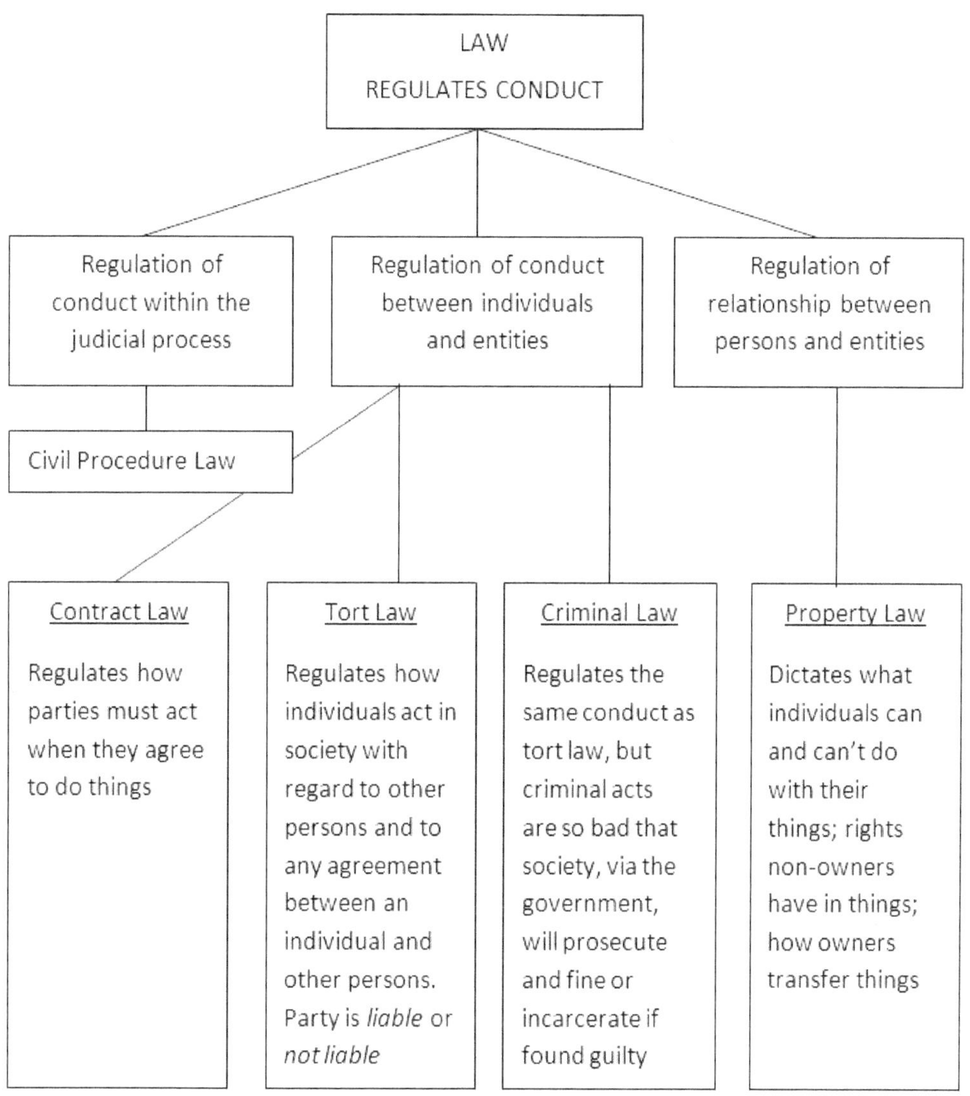
LAW
REGULATES CONDUCT
Regulation of conduct within the judicial process
Regulation of conduct between individuals and entities
Regulation of relationship between persons and entities
Civil Procedure Law
Contract Law
Regulates how parties must act when they agree to do things
Tort Law
Regulates how individuals act in society with regard to other persons and to any agreement between an individual and other persons. Party is liable or not liable
Criminal Law
Regulates the same conduct as tort law, but criminal acts are so bad that society, via the government, will prosecute and fine or incarcerate if found guilty
Property Law
Dictates what individuals can and can't do with their things; rights non-owners have in things; how owners transfer things

Sources of United States law

The foundational source of law in the United States is the U.S. Constitution, which establishes the federal government and enumerates its powers. The U.S. Constitution is *the supreme law of the land.* Therefore, any local, state, or federal law conflicting with the Constitution is void and unenforceable.

Powers not given to the federal government are reserved to the states. State constitutions establish state governments and enumerate their powers.

Treaties are international agreements entered into with other countries, executed by the President with *advice and consent* from the Senate.

Statutes and *ordinances* are codified laws and are created by legislative bodies. Statutes are interpreted and enforced by two types of agency action.

>*Rulemaking* – the adoption of rules and regulations by the agency defining the requirements of a statute. For example, the definition of gross income under the statute is less than one page, but the IRS regulations for this term are dozens of pages.

>*Decisionmaking* – agencies resolve disputes arising under the rules, regulations, and authorizing statute.

Codified laws establish courses of conduct that covered parties must follow. They are written laws (i.e., statutes) enacted by the legislative branch to define acceptable conduct by its citizens. For example, U.S. Congress empowered the commerce clause to regulate commerce between the states and with the Indian nations (e.g., antitrust, bankruptcy). The state legislature has similar power to regulate activity within its borders (e.g., workers compensation, uniform commercial, licenses). State legislatures delegate some power to municipalities, school districts, and others. (e.g., ordinances for building codes, zoning, traffic).

Administrative rules and regulations come from bureaucracies created by the legislative and executive branches of government. Agencies interpret and enforce statutes enacted by legislation (e.g., Congress enacted a statute authorizing the collection of income taxes). For example, the IRS is the administrative agency charged with interpreting and enforcing the income tax statute.

Executive orders are issued by the President and state governors and regulate the conduct of those on whom the executive orders are focused.

Judicial decisions are written opinions of a judge or justice deciding the dispute before setting forth the reasons for the decision. These decisions resolve the dispute and serve as a precedent for the resolution of a future similar dispute. Judicial decisions are often created by appellate courts that resolve legal controversies. An appellate court issues decisions that state the holding of the case and the rationale used by the court in reaching that decision.

Priority of law in the United States

1) U.S. Constitution takes precedence over all other laws (i.e., *the supreme law of the land*).

2) Federal statutes take precedence over federal regulations.

3) Federal law takes precedence over state law, where the state law conflicts.

4) State constitution represents the highest authority in the state, state statutes, then state regulations.

Values-based law

Moral values address fundamental questions of right and wrong. For example, laws against murder protect life. However, not every immoral act breaks the law (e.g., lying to a friend).

Economic values address the accumulation, preservation, use, and distribution of wealth. For example, laws against shoplifting protect property. In addition, the law encourages homeownership by giving tax benefits to incentivize people to borrow and buy a home.

Political values address the relationship between government and individuals (e.g., voting, criminal law).

Social values address issues important to society (e.g., free public education).

Many laws combine values. For example, consider laws against theft. The laws address *moral* (e.g., stealing), *economic* (e.g., protection of property), *political* (punishment for violating criminal statutes), and *social issues* (e.g., respecting the property of others).

The doctrine of *stare decisis*

Court decisions become guidance or precedent for future cases. Lower courts must follow precedent set by higher courts.

The precedent of another jurisdiction does not bind courts in other jurisdictions.

Adherence to *stare decisis* promotes uniformity and predictability of the legal system.

Constitution of the United States of America

U.S. Constitution established a form of the federal government with three branches:

1) Legislative to enact laws – Congress consists of the House of Representatives and Senate.

2) Executive to enforce the laws – President, Vice President, and administrative agencies.

3) Judicial to interpret and determine the validity of laws – courts.

Powers given to the federal government are enumerated or designated powers set forth in the Constitution. All other powers not enumerated in the Constitution are reserved for the states. The emphasis is to protect the rights of individuals (i.e., civil liberties).

Federalism and delegated powers

Federalism – the power to govern is shared by one central or federal government and the 50 states

Delegated (or Enumerated) Powers – those powers set forth in the Constitution assigned to the federal government. Enumerated powers authorize the federal government to regulate specific national and international affairs.

Reserved Powers – those powers not delegated to the federal government are reserved for the states.

The doctrine of separation of powers

Article I establishes a bicameral legislature – establishes Congress.

1) House of Representatives, where each state has representation based on population.

2) Senate, where each state is represented equally with two Senators.

Article II establishes the offices of the President and Vice President and describes requirements and how elected.

Article III establishes a judiciary to hear and resolve legal disputes.

Checks and balances

Checks and balances are included in the federal government system so that no branch becomes too powerful.

1) Judiciary may examine the acts of the Congress and President to determine whether they comply with Constitution provisions.

2) President enters treaties with foreign nations with the advice and consent of the Senate.

Supremacy clause

The Constitution, treaties, federal laws, and regulations are the supreme law of the land.

To the extent state and local laws conflict with federal law, they are preempted.

Some areas of governance are exclusively the federal government's (e.g., postage, coining money, national defense).

Some areas of governance are concurrent where both the state and federal governments share powers (e.g., environmental protection).

Commerce clause

Congress granted the power to regulate trade with foreign governments, between states, and with the Indian nations.

Native Americans

1) At the time of its founding, the colonies (states), in the U.S. Constitution, delegated to the federal government the authority to regulate commerce with the Indian tribes.

2) Applicable to the original thirteen states and the territory to become the United States of America.

Foreign Commerce

1) Federal government has the exclusive power to regulate commerce with foreign nations.

2) Typically through treaties negotiated and signed by the President with the consent of the Senate.

Interstate Commerce

1) Federal government the authority to regulate interstate commerce.

2) Originally interpreted, this clause means commerce that moved in interstate commerce.

3) Modern rule allows the federal government to regulate activities that affect interstate commerce.

4) This test subjects a substantial amount of business activity in the United States to federal regulation.

State Police Power

1) The retained powers of the states to govern within their borders are police power

2) The power to enact legislation for health, safety, welfare, morals, and aesthetics.

3) Includes those powers delegated to local municipalities (e.g., building regulations, zoning codes).

Dormant commerce clause

Prohibits state legislation that discriminates against interstate commerce.

Bill of Rights and other Amendments

The Bill of Rights is the first ten Amendments to the U.S. Constitution ratified in 1791 and guarantying fundamental rights reserved for the people.

Freedom of speech

The First Amendment *freedom of speech* protects the right of individuals to speak freely.

The first Amendment divides speech into three categories.

1) Fully protected speech is political speech (e.g., oral, written, symbolic) that the government may not prohibit or regulate (e.g., flag burning).

2) Limited protected speech: may not be prohibited but may be regulated for time, place, and manner.

    a.   Offensive speech may be regulated (i.e., FCC regulation of radio and television programs).

    b.   Commercial speech such as advertising cannot be prohibited but may be restricted to placement for safety or aesthetic reasons.

3) Unprotected speech: may be prohibited or banned by the government.

    a.   Common examples include yelling "fire!" in a crowded place, fighting words, and defamation.

    b.   One complicated issue to define is obscenity; what may be obscene may be acceptable to another.

    c.   Obscene speech is a category of speech unprotected by the First Amendment.

    d.   Obscenity laws prohibit lewd, filthy, or disgusting words or pictures.

Free speech in cyberspace

The Supreme Court held that the Internet be given the highest level of First Amendment free-speech protections.

As a participatory form of mass speech, the Internet deserves the highest protection from government intrusion.

Because the Internet is a global medium, there is no way to prevent indecent material from abroad.

Freedom of religion

The Establishment clause prohibits the federal government from establishing a state religion and has been interpreted to prohibit promoting one religion over another.

The Free Exercise clause prohibits the federal government from interfering with the rights of the individual to worship as desired unless it involves human or animal sacrifice.

Due process clause

No person shall be deprived of life, liberty, or property without due process of law.

Due process applies to the federal government (via the 5th Amendment) and the state and local governments (via the 14th Amendment).

Substantive due process:

1) Requires that laws enacted by the government be clear on their face and not overly broad.

2) Test whether a "reasonable person" could understand the law to comply with it.

Procedural due process:

The government must give notice and a hearing (i.e., opportunity to be heard) to the individual of legal action taken against them.

Equal protection clause

Prohibits state, local and federal governments from denying persons equal protection of the law.

Laws that classify and treat similarly situated persons differently violate the equal protection clause.

Three levels of tests developed by the Supreme Court to address equal protection and what has come to be known as the anti-discrimination provision of the Constitution

Strict scrutiny – a regulation that classifies individuals based upon a suspect class (race) generally will not be found constitutional (e.g., granting federal benefit to one race violates Equal Protection).

Intermediate scrutiny – regulation related to protected classes (age or sex) will be permissible so long as reasonably related to a legitimate government purpose (e.g., requiring government engineers to be men violates Equal Protection).

Rational basis – regulations of classes other than suspect and protected will be permissible where the is a justifiable reason for the law (e.g., subsidies to a farmer).

Notes for active learning

U.S. Court Systems – Federal and State Courts

There are two kinds of courts in the USA – federal courts and state courts.

Federal courts are established under the U.S. Constitution by Congress to decide disputes involving the Constitution and laws passed by Congress. A state establishes state and local courts (within states, local courts are established by cities, counties, and other municipalities).

Jurisdiction of federal and state courts

The differences between federal courts and state courts are defined by jurisdiction.[1] Jurisdiction refers to the kinds of cases that a particular court is authorized to hear and adjudicate (i.e., the pronouncement of a legally binding judgment upon the parties to the dispute).

Federal court jurisdiction is limited to the types of cases listed in the Constitution and specifically provided by Congress. For the most part, federal courts only hear:

- cases in which the United States is a party[2];

- cases involving violations of the U.S. Constitution or federal laws (under federal-question jurisdiction[3]);

- cases between citizens of different states if the amount in controversy *exceeds* $75,000 (under diversity jurisdiction[4]); and

- bankruptcy, copyright, patent, and maritime law cases.

State courts, in contrast, have broad jurisdiction, so the cases individual citizens are likely to be involved in (e.g., robberies, traffic violations, contracts, and family disputes) are usually heard and decided in state courts. The only cases state courts are not allowed to hear are lawsuits against the United States and those involving certain specific federal laws: criminal, antitrust, bankruptcy, patent, copyright, and some maritime law cases.

In many cases, both federal and state courts have jurisdiction whereby the plaintiff (i.e., the party initiating the suit) can choose whether to file their claim in state or federal court.

Criminal cases involving federal laws can be tried only in federal court, but most criminal cases involve violations of state law and are tried in state court. Robbery is a crime, but what law makes it is a crime? Except for certain exceptions, state laws, not federal laws, make robbery a crime. There are only a few federal laws about robbery, such as the law that makes it a federal crime to rob a bank whose deposits are insured by a federal agency. Examples of other federal crimes are the transport of illegal drugs into the country or across state lines and using the U.S. mail system to defraud consumers.

Crimes committed on federal property (e.g., national parks or military reservations) are prosecuted in federal court.

Federal courts may hear cases concerning state laws if the issue is whether the state law violates the federal Constitution. Suppose a state law forbids slaughtering animals outside of certain limited areas. A neighborhood association brings a case in state court against a defendant who sacrifices chickens in their backyard. When the court issues an order (i.e., an injunction[5]) forbidding the defendant from further sacrifices, the defendant challenges the state law in federal court as an unconstitutional infringement of religious freedom.

Some conduct is illegal under both federal and state laws. For example, federal laws prohibit employment discrimination, and the states have added additional legal restrictions. A person can file their claim in either federal or state court under federal law or federal and state laws. A case that only involves a state law can be brought only in state court.

Appeals for review of actions by federal administrative agencies are federal civil cases.

For example, if the Environmental Protection Agency, over the objection of area residents, issued a permit to a paper mill to discharge water used in its milling process into the Scenic River, the residents may appeal and have the federal court of appeals review the agency's decision.

---

[1] *jurisdiction* – 1) the legal authority of a court to hear and decide specific types of case; 2) the geographic area over which the court has the authority to decide cases.

[2] *parties* – the plaintiff and the defendant in a lawsuit.

[3] *federal-question jurisdiction* – the federal district courts' authorization to hear and decide cases arising under the Constitution, laws, or treaties of the United States.

[4] *diversity jurisdiction* – the federal district courts' authority to hear and decide civil cases involving plaintiffs and defendants who are citizens of different states (or U.S. citizens and foreign nationals) and meet specific statutory requirements.

[5] *injunction* – a judge's order that a party takes or refrain from taking a particular action. An injunction may be preliminary until the outcome of a case is determined or permanent.

Organization of the federal courts

Congress has divided the country into 94 federal judicial districts, with each having a U.S. district court. The U.S. district courts are the federal trial courts -- where federal cases are tried, witnesses testify, and juries serve.

Each district has a U.S. bankruptcy court, which is part of the district court that administers the U.S. bankruptcy laws.

Congress uses state boundaries to help define the districts. Some districts cover an entire state, like Idaho. Other districts cover just part of a state, like the Northern District of California. Congress placed each of the ninety-four districts in one of twelve regional circuits whereby each circuit has a court of appeals. The losing party can petition the court of appeals to review the case to determine if the district judge applied the law correctly.

There is a U.S. Court of Appeals for the Federal Circuit, whose jurisdiction is defined by subject matter rather than geography. It hears appeals from certain courts and agencies, such as the U.S. Court of International Trade, the U.S. Court of Federal Claims, and the U.S. Patent and Trademark Office, and certain types of cases from the district courts (mainly lawsuits claiming that patents have been infringed).

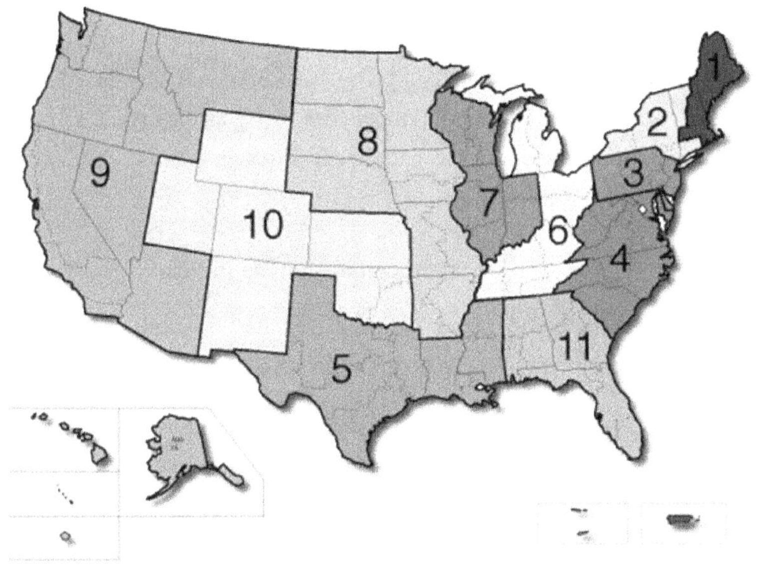

Twelve regional federal circuits

The Supreme Court in Washington, D.C., is the highest court in the nation. The losing party can petition in a case in the court of appeals (or, sometimes, in a state supreme court), can petition the Supreme Court to hear an appeal.

Unlike a court of appeals, the Supreme Court does not have to hear the case. The Supreme Court hears only a small percentage of the cases it is asked to review.

The importance of judicial independence

The founders of the United States recognized that the judicial branch must remain independent to fulfill its mission effectively and impartially. Article III of the Constitution protects certain types of judges by providing that they serve "during good behavior" and prohibits the reduction of their salary.

These constitutional protections allow judges to make unpopular decisions without fear of losing their jobs or having their pay cut.

For example, the Supreme Court's decision in *Brown v. Board of Education* in 1954 declared racial segregation in public schools to be unconstitutional. This decision was unpopular with large segments of society at that time. Some members of Congress even wanted to replace the judges who made the decision, but this Constitutional protection would not allow them to do so.

Article III judges

"Article III judge" denotes federal judges who under Article III of the Constitution are enabled to exercise "the judicial power of the United States" without fear of losing their jobs. They serve for "good Behaviour," which means they can be removed from office only by the rare impeachment and conviction process.

Article III further provides that their compensation cannot be reduced. From a practical standpoint, almost all of these judges hold office for as long as they wish. "Article III judges" are those on the U.S. Supreme Court, the federal courts of appeals and district courts, and the U.S. Court of International Trade.

Constitutional protections for the judiciary

Federal judges appointed under Article III of the Constitution are guaranteed what amounts to life tenure and a fixed salary, not to be afraid to make an unpopular decision.

For example, in *Gregg v. Georgia*, the Supreme Court said it is constitutional for the federal and state governments to impose the death penalty if the statute is carefully drafted to provide adequate safeguards. Even though some people are opposed to the death penalty, Article III protections allowed the Judge to decide without fear of reciprocity.

The constitutional protection that gives federal judges the freedom and independence to make decisions politically and socially unpopular is a fundamental element of our democracy.

According to the Declaration of Independence, one reason the American colonies wanted to separate from England was that King George III "made judges dependent on his/her will alone, for the tenure of their offices, and the amount and payment of their salaries."

Federal judges other than enumerated in Article III

Bankruptcy judges and magistrate judges conduct some of the proceedings held in federal courts. Bankruptcy judges handle almost all bankruptcy matters in bankruptcy courts technically included in the district courts but function as separate entities.

Magistrate judges carry out various responsibilities in the district courts and often help prepare the district judges' cases for trial. They also may preside over criminal misdemeanor trials and may preside over civil trials when both parties agree to have the case heard by a magistrate judge instead of a district judge.

Unlike district judges, bankruptcy and magistrate judges do not exercise "the judicial power of the United States" but perform duties delegated to them by district judges. Bankruptcy and magistrate judges serve for fourteen and eight-year terms, respectively, rather than "during good Behaviour."

Bankruptcy judges and magistrate judges don't have the same protections as judges appointed under Article III of the Constitution. Bankruptcy judges, in contrast, may be removed from office by circuit judicial councils, and magistrate judges may be removed by the district judges of the magistrate judge's district.

Courts and judges

Congress authorizes a set number of judge positions, or judgeships, for each court level. Since the 1869 "Circuit Judges Act," Congress mandated that the Supreme Court would consist of 9 justices. As of 2021, it had mandated 179 court of appeals judgeships and 678 district court judgeships. (In 1950, there were 65 courts of appeals and 212 district judgeships).

As of 2018, Congress mandated 350 bankruptcy judgeships and about 551 full-time and part-time magistrate judgeships. All judgeships are rarely filled at any one time as judges die or retire, causing vacancies until judges are appointed to replace them. In addition to judges in these positions, retired judges continue to perform some judicial work.

Federal judges and judgeships

Supreme Court justices and the court of appeals and district judges are appointed to office by the President, with the approval of the U.S. Senate. Presidents most often appoint judges who are members, or at least supportive, of their political party, but that does not mean that judges are given appointments solely for partisan reasons.

The professional qualifications of prospective federal judges are rigorously evaluated by the Department of Justice (DOJ), which consults with others, such as lawyers who can evaluate the prospect's abilities. The Senate Judiciary Committee undertakes a separate examination of the nominees.

Magistrate judges and bankruptcy judges are not appointed by the President or subject to Congress's approval. The court of appeals in each circuit appoints bankruptcy judges for fourteen-year terms. District courts appoint magistrate judges for eight-year terms.

Qualifications for becoming a federal judge

Although there are almost no formal qualifications for federal judges, there are some informal ones. For example, while magistrate judges and bankruptcy judges are required by statute to be lawyers, there is no requirement that district judges, circuit judges, or Supreme Court justices be lawyers.

However, there is no legal precedent for a president to nominate someone who is not a lawyer. Before their appointment, most judges were private attorneys, but many were judges in state courts or other federal courts. Some were government attorneys, and a few were law professors.

Ethical standards for judges

Judges follow the ethical standards set out in the *Code of Conduct for United States Judges*, which contains guidelines to help them avoid situations that might limit their ability to be fair--or that might make it appear to others that their fairness is in question. It tells them, for example, to be careful not to do anything that might cause people to think they would favor one side in a case over another, such as giving speeches that urge voters to pick one candidate over another for public office or asking people to contribute money to civic organizations.

Additionally, Congress has enacted laws telling judges to withdraw or recuse themselves from any case in which a close relative is a party or in which they have any financial interest, even one share of stock.

Congress requires judges to file an annual financial disclosure form, so that their stock holdings, board memberships, and other financial interests are a matter of public record.

Congress has also enacted a law that allows anyone to file a complaint alleging that a judge (other than a Supreme Court justice) has engaged in conduct "prejudicial to the effective and expeditious administration of the business of the courts" or that a judge has a mental or physical disability that makes him/her unable to discharge the duties of the office adequately.

A complaint is filed with the clerk of the court of appeals of the judge's circuit and considered by the chief judge of the court of appeals. If the chief judge believes the complaint deserves attention, the chief judge appoints a special committee of the circuit judicial council to investigate.

If the committee concludes that the complaint is valid, it may recommend various actions, such as temporarily removing the judge from hearing cases, but it may not recommend that an Article III judge be removed from office. Only Congress may do that, through the impeachment process.

Chief Judges dismiss the great majority of complaints filed under this law because the complaints involve judges' decisions in particular cases. This law may not be used to complain about decisions, even what may appear to be a very wrong decision or very unfair treatment of a party in a case.

Parties in a lawsuit who believe the judge issued an incorrect ruling may appeal the case to a higher court, under the rules of procedure.

Senior judge status

Most federal judges retire from full-time service at around sixty-five or seventy years of age and become senior judges. Senior judges are still federal judges, eligible to earn their full salary and to continue hearing cases if they and their colleagues want them to do so, but they usually maintain a reduced caseload.

Full-time judges are known as active judges.

Docket assignments

Each court, with more than one judge, must determine a procedure for assigning cases to judges.

Most district and bankruptcy courts use random assignment, which helps to ensure a fair distribution of cases and prevents "judge shopping," which refers to parties' attempts to have their cases heard by the judge whom they believe will act most favorably.

Other courts assign cases by rotation, subject matter, or geographic division of the court.

In courts of appeals, cases are usually assigned by random means to temporary three-judge panels.

Notes for active learning

How Civil Cases Move Through the Federal Courts

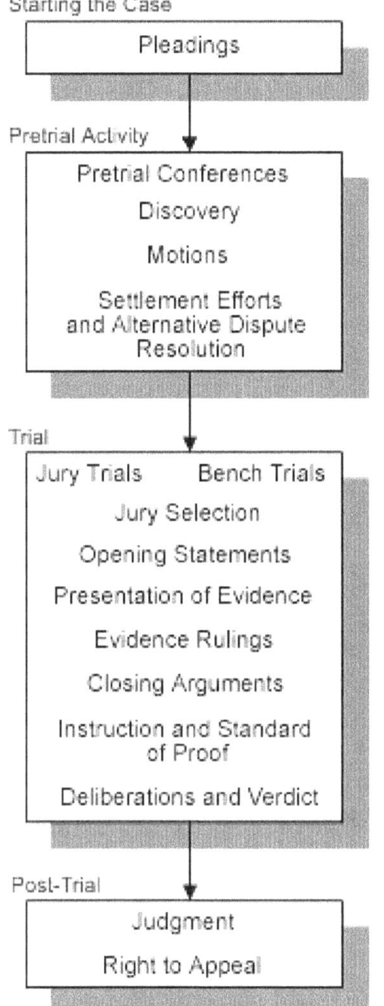

A federal civil case begins when a person, or their legal representative, files a paper with the clerk of the court that asserts another person's wrongful act injured the person. In legal terminology, the plaintiff files a *complaint* against the defendant.

The defendant files an *answer* to the complaint. These written statements of the party's positions are called pleadings. In some circumstances, the defendant may file a *motion* instead of an answer; the motion asks the court to take some action, such as dismiss the case or require the plaintiff to explain more clearly what the lawsuit is about.

Jury trials

In a jury trial, the jury decides what happened, and to apply the legal standards, the judge tells them to apply to reach a verdict. The plaintiff presents evidence supporting its view of the case, and the defendant presents evidence rebutting the plaintiff's evidence or supporting its view of the case. From these presentations, the jury must decide what happened and applied the law to those facts.

The jury never decides what law applies to the case; that is the role of the judge. For example, in a discrimination case where the plaintiff alleged that their workplace was hostile, the judge tells the jury the legal standard for a hostile environment.

The jury would have to decide whether the plaintiff's description of events was true and whether those events met the legal standard. A trial jury, or petit jury, may consist of six to twelve jurors in a civil case.

Bench trials

If the parties agree not to have a *jury trial* and leave the fact-finding to the judge, the trial is a *bench trial*. In bench and jury trials, the judge ensures the correct legal standards are followed.

In contrast to a jury trial, the judge decides the facts and renders the verdict in a *bench trial*.

For example, in a discrimination case in which the plaintiff alleged a hostile environment, the judge would determine the legal standard for a hostile environment and decide whether the plaintiff's description of events was true and whether those events met the legal standard.

Some kinds of cases always have bench trials. For example, there is never a jury trial if the plaintiff is seeking an injunction, an order from the judge that the defendant does, or stop doing something, as opposed to monetary damages.

Some statutes provide that a judge must decide the facts in certain types of cases.

Jury selection

A jury trial begins with the selection of jurors. Citizens are selected for jury service through a process set out in laws passed by Congress and in the federal rules of procedure.

First, citizens are called to court to be available to serve on juries. These citizens are selected at random from sources, in most districts, lists of registered voters, which may be augmented by other sources, such as lists of licensed drivers in the judicial district.

The judge and the lawyers choose who will serve on the jury.

To choose the jurors, the judge and sometimes the lawyers ask prospective jurors questions to determine if they will decide the case fairly, a process known as *voir dire*.

The lawyers may request that the judge excuse jurors they think may not be impartial, such as those who know a party in the case or who have had an experience that might make them favor one side over the other. These requests for rejecting jurors are *challenges for cause*.

The lawyers may request that the judge excuse a certain number of jurors without reason; these requests are *peremptory challenges*.

Instructions and standard of proof

Following the closing arguments, the judge gives instructions to the jury, explaining the relevant law, how the law applies to the case, and what questions the jury must decide.

How sure do jurors have to be before they reach a verdict? One important instruction the judge gives the jury is the standard of proof they must follow in deciding the case.

The courts, through their decisions, and Congress, through statutes, have established standards by which facts must be proven in criminal and civil cases.

In civil cases, to decide for the plaintiff, the jury must determine by a *preponderance of the evidence* that the defendant failed to perform a legal duty and violated the plaintiff's rights. A preponderance of the evidence means that, based on the evidence, the evidence favors the plaintiff more (even if only slightly) than it favors the defendant.

If the evidence in favor of the plaintiff could be placed on one side of a scale and that in favor of the defendant on the other, the plaintiff would win if the evidence in favor of the plaintiff was heavy enough to tip the scale. If the two sides were even, or if the scale tipped for the defendant, the defendant would win.

Judgment

In civil cases, if the jury (or judge) decides in favor of the plaintiff, the result usually is that the defendant must pay the plaintiff money or damages. The judge orders the defendant to pay the decided amount. Sometimes the defendant is ordered to take some specific action that will restore the plaintiff's rights. If the defendant wins the case, there is nothing more the trial court needs to do as the case is disposed of and the defendant is held not liable.

Right to appeal

The losing party in a federal civil case has a right to appeal the verdict to the U.S. court of appeals (i.e., Federal Circuit Courts) and ask the court to review the case to determine whether the trial was conducted properly. The losing party in the state trial court has a right to appeal the verdict to the state court of appeal.

The grounds for appeal usually are that the federal district (or state) judge made an error, either in the procedure (e.g., admitting improper evidence) or interpreting the law. The government may appeal in civil cases, as any other party may. Neither party may appeal if there was no trial -- parties settled their civil case out of court.

Notes for active learning

How Criminal Cases Move Through the Federal Courts

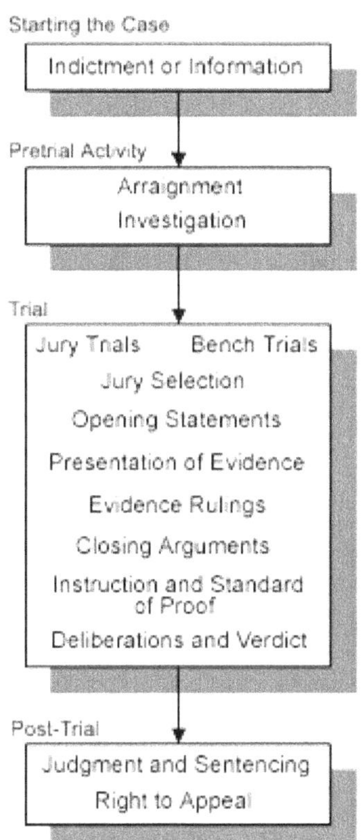

Indictment or information

A criminal case formally begins with an indictment or information, which is a formal accusation that a person committed a crime.

An indictment may be obtained when a lawyer (i.e., prosecutor) for the executive branch of the U.S. government (i.e., U.S. attorney or assistant U.S. attorney) present evidence to a federal grand jury that, according to the government, indicates a person committed a crime.

The U.S. attorney tries to convince the grand jury that there is enough evidence to show that the person probably committed the crime and should be formally accused. If the grand jury agrees, it issues an indictment.

A grand jury is different from a trial jury or petit jury.

A grand jury determines whether the person may be tried for a crime; a petit jury listens to the evidence presented at the trial and determines whether the defendant is guilty.

Petit is French for "small"; petit juries usually consist of twelve jurors in criminal cases.

Grand is French for "large"; grand juries have from sixteen to twenty-three jurors.

Grand jury indictments are most often used for *felonies* (i.e., punishable by imprisonment of more than a year or by death) such as bank robberies or sales of illegal drugs.

Grand jury indictments are not necessary to prosecute *misdemeanors* (i.e., less serious than a felony but more serious than an infraction) and are necessary for felonies.

For lesser crimes, the U.S. attorney issues an *information* that substitutes for an indictment. For example, speeding on a highway in a national park is a misdemeanor.

An information is used when a defendant waives an indictment by a grand jury.

Arraignment

After the grand jury issues the indictment, the accused (i.e., defendant) is summoned to court or arrested (if not already in custody). The next step is an arraignment, a proceeding in which the defendant is brought before a judge, told of the charges they are accused of, and asked to plead guilty or not guilty. If the defendant's plea is guilty, a time is set for the defendant to return to court to be sentenced.

If the defendant pleads "not guilty," the time is set for the trial.

A defendant may enter a plea bargain with the prosecution--usually by agreeing to plead guilty to some but not all charges or lesser charges. The prosecution drops the remaining charges.

About nine out of ten defendants in criminal cases plead guilty.

Investigation

In a criminal case, a defense lawyer conducts a thorough investigation before trial, interviewing witnesses, visiting the crime scene, and examining physical evidence. An important part of this investigation is determining whether the evidence the government plans to use to prove its case was obtained legally.

The Fourth Amendment to the Constitution forbids unreasonable searches and seizures. To enforce this protection, the Supreme Court has decided that illegally seized evidence cannot be used at trial for most purposes.

For example, if the police seize evidence from a defendant's home without a search warrant, the lawyer for the defendant can ask the court to exclude the evidence from use at trial. The court holds a hearing to determine whether the search was unreasonable.

If the court rules that key evidence was seized illegally and cannot be used, the government often drops the charges against the defendant.

If the government has a strong case and the court ruled that the evidence was obtained legally, the defendant may decide to plead guilty rather than go to trial, where a conviction is likely.

Deliberations and verdict

After receiving its instructions from the judge, the jury retires to the jury room to discuss the evidence and reach a verdict (a decision on the factual issues). A criminal jury verdict must be unanimous; all jurors must agree that the defendant is guilty or not guilty.

If the jurors cannot agree, the judge declares a mistrial, and the prosecutor must decide whether to ask the court to dismiss the case or have it presented to another jury.

Judgment and sentencing

In federal criminal cases, if the jury (or judge, if there is no jury) decides that the defendant is guilty, the judge sets a date for a sentencing hearing. In federal criminal cases, the jury does not decide whether the defendant will go to prison or for how long; the judge does.

In federal death penalty cases, the jury does decide whether the defendant will receive a death sentence. Sentencing statutes passed by Congress control the judge's sentencing decision. Additionally, judges use Sentencing Guidelines, issued by the U.S. Sentencing Commission, as a source of advice as to the proper sentence. The guidelines consider the nature of the offense and the offender's criminal history.

A presentence report, prepared by one of the court's probation officers, provides the judge with information about the offender and the offense, including the sentence recommended by the guidelines. After determining the sentence, the judge signs a judgment, including the plea, the verdict, and sentence.

Right to appeal

A defendant who is found guilty in a federal criminal trial has a right to appeal the decision to the U.S. court of appeals, that is, ask the court of appeals to review the case to determine whether the trial was conducted properly. The grounds for appeal are usually that the district judge is said to have made an error, either in a procedure (admitting improper evidence, for example) or interpreting the law.

A defendant who pled guilty may not appeal the conviction.

A defendant who pled guilty may have the right to appeal their sentence.

The government may not appeal if a defendant in a criminal case is found not guilty because the Double Jeopardy Clause of the Fifth Amendment to the Constitution provides that no person shall "be twice put in jeopardy of life or limb" for the same offense.

This reflects society's belief that, even if a subsequent trial might finally find a defendant guilty, it is not proper for the government to harass an acquitted defendant through repeated retrials.

However, the government may sometimes appeal a sentence.

Notes for active learning

How Civil and Criminal Appeals Move Through the Federal Courts

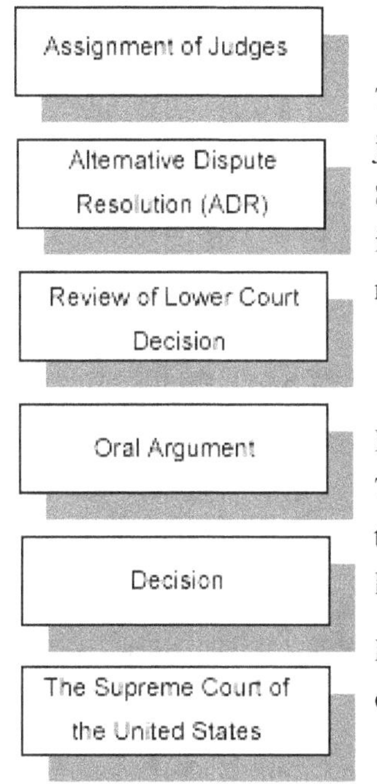

Assignment of judges

The courts of appeals usually assign cases to a panel of three judges. The panel decides the case for the entire court. Sometimes, when the parties request it or a question of unusual importance, the judges on the appeals court assemble *en banc* (a rare event).

Review of a lower court decision

In making its decision, the panel reviews key parts of the record. The record consists of the documents filed in the case at trial and the transcript of the trial proceedings. The panel learns about the lawyers' legal arguments from the lawyers' briefs.

Briefs are written documents that each side submits to explain its case and tell why the court should decide in its favor.

Oral argument

If the court permits oral argument, the lawyers for each side have a limited amount of time (typically between 15 to 30 minutes) to argue (i.e., advocate and explain) their case to the judges (or justices at the highest court in the jurisdiction) in a formal courtroom session. The judges (or justices for the highest court in the jurisdiction) frequently question the attorneys about the relevant law as it applies to the facts and issues in the case before them.

A court of appeals differs from the federal trial courts. There are no jurors, witnesses, or court reporters. The lawyers for each side, but not the parties, are usually present in the courtroom.

Decision

After the submission of briefs and oral arguments, the judges discuss the case privately, consider relevant *precedents* (court decisions from higher courts in prior cases with similar facts and legal issues), and reach a decision. Courts are required to follow precedents.

For example, a U.S. court of appeals must follow the U.S. Supreme Court's decisions; a district court must follow the decisions of the U.S. Supreme Court and the decisions of the court of appeals of its circuit.

Courts are influenced by decisions they are not required to follow, such as the decisions of other circuits. Courts follow precedent unless they set forth reasons for the diversion.

At least two of the three judges on the panel must agree on a decision. One judge who agrees with the decision is chosen to write an opinion, which announces and explains the decision.

If a judge on the panel disagrees with the majority's opinion, the judge may write a dissent, giving reasons for disagreeing.

Many appellate opinions are published in books of opinions, called reporters. The opinions are read carefully by other judges and lawyers looking for precedents to guide them in their cases.

The accumulated judicial opinions make up a body of law known as *case law*, which is usually an accurate predictor of how future cases will be decided.

For decisions that the judges believe are important to the parties and contribute little to the law, the appeals courts frequently use short, unsigned opinions that often are not published.

If the court of appeals decides that the trial judge incorrectly interpreted the law or followed incorrect procedures, it reverses the district court's decision.

For example, the court of appeals could hold that the district judge allowed the jury to base its decision on evidence that never should have been admitted, and thus the defendant cannot be guilty.

Most of the time, courts of appeals uphold, rather than the reverse, district court decisions.

Sometimes when a higher court reverses the decision of the district court, it sends the case back (i.e., *remand* the case) to the lower court for another trial.

For example, *Miranda v. Arizona* case (1966), the Supreme Court ruled 5-4 that Ernesto Miranda's confession could not be used as evidence because he had not been advised of his right to remain silent or of his right to have a lawyer present during questioning.

However, the government did have other evidence against him. The case was remanded for a new trial, in which the improperly obtained confession was not used as evidence, but the other evidence convicted Miranda.

The Supreme Court of the United States

The Supreme Court is the highest in the nation. It is a different kind of appeals court; its major function is not correcting errors made by trial judges but clarifying the law in cases of national importance or when lower courts disagree about interpreting the Constitution or federal laws.

The Supreme Court does not have to hear every case that it is asked to review. Each year, losing parties ask the Supreme Court to review about 8,000 cases.

Almost all cases come to the Court as a *petition for writ of certiorari*. The court selects only about 80 to 120 of the most significant cases to review with oral arguments.

Supreme Court decisions establish a precedent for interpreting the Constitution and federal laws; holdings that state and federal courts must follow.

The power of judicial review makes the Supreme Court's role in our government vital. Judicial review is the power of a court when deciding a case to declare that a law passed by a legislature or action by the executive branch is invalid because it is inconsistent with the Constitution.

Although district courts, courts of appeals, and state courts can exercise the power of judicial review, their decisions about federal law are always subject, on appeal, to review by the Supreme Court.

When the Supreme Court declares a law unconstitutional, its decision can only be overruled by a later decision of the Supreme Court or Amendment to the Constitution.

Seven of the twenty-seven Amendments to the Constitution have invalidated the decisions of the Supreme Court. However, most Supreme Court cases do not concern the constitutionality of laws, but the interpretation of laws passed by Congress.

Although Congress has steadily increased the number of district and appeals court judges over the years, the Supreme Court has remained the same size since 1869. It consists of a Chief Justice and eight associate justices.

Like the federal court of appeals and federal district judges, the Supreme Court justices are appointed by the President with the Senate's *advice and consent.*

Unlike the judges in the courts of appeals, Supreme Court justices never sit on panels. Absent recusal, nine justices hear cases, and a majority ruling decides cases.

The Supreme Court begins its annual session, or term, on the first Monday of October. The term lasts until the Court has announced its decisions in cases where it has heard an argument that term—usually late June or early July.

During the term, the Court, sitting for two weeks at a time, hears oral arguments on Monday through Wednesday and holds private conferences to discuss the cases, reach decisions, and begin preparing the written opinions that explain its decisions.

Most decisions and opinions are released in the late spring and early summer.

Notes for active learning

Standards of review for federal courts

Standard of review	*De novo*	Clearly erroneous	Abuse of discretion
Type of decision under review	Question of the law	Question of fact	Discretionary action
Lower-court decision maker	Trial judge	Trial judge	Trial judge
Deference given to lower court	No deference	Substantial deference	Extreme deference
Party typically benefitted	Appellant	Appellee	Appellee
Definition	An appellate court reviews the legal question anew and independently, without regard to the conclusions reached by the trial court. "When *de novo* review is compelled, no form of appellate deference is acceptable." *Salve Regina College v. Russell*, (1991).	A finding is 'clearly erroneous' when although there is evidence to support it, the reviewing court on the entire evidence is left with the definite and firm conviction that a mistake has been committed. *United States v. United States Gypsum Co.*, (1948) "If the district court's account of the evidence is plausible in light of the record viewed in its entirety, the court of appeals may not reverse it even though convinced that had it been sitting as the trier of fact, it would have weighed the evidence differently. When there are two permissible views of the evidence, the factfinder's choice between them cannot be clearly erroneous." *Anderson v. Bessemer City*, (1985).	Generally, an abuse of discretion only occurs where no reasonable person could take the view adopted by the trial court. If reasonable persons could differ, no abuse of discretion can be found. *Harrington v. DeVito*, (7th Cir.1981) Under the abuse of discretion standard, a trial court's decision will not be disturbed unless the appellate court has a definite and firm conviction that the lower court made a clear error of judgment or exceeded the bounds of permissible choice in the circumstances. We will not alter a trial court's decision unless it can be shown that the court's decision was an arbitrary, capricious, whimsical, or manifestly unreasonable judgment. *Wright v. Abbott Laboratories, Inc.*, (10th Cir. 2001)
Examples	Motions for summary judgment, constitutional questions, statutory interpretation	Questions regarding who did what, where, and when: questions of intent and motive: questions of ultimate fact (such as negligence)	Rule 11 sanctions, attorney's fees, courtroom management, motions to compel, injunctions, and temporary restraining orders.

The Massachusetts Court System

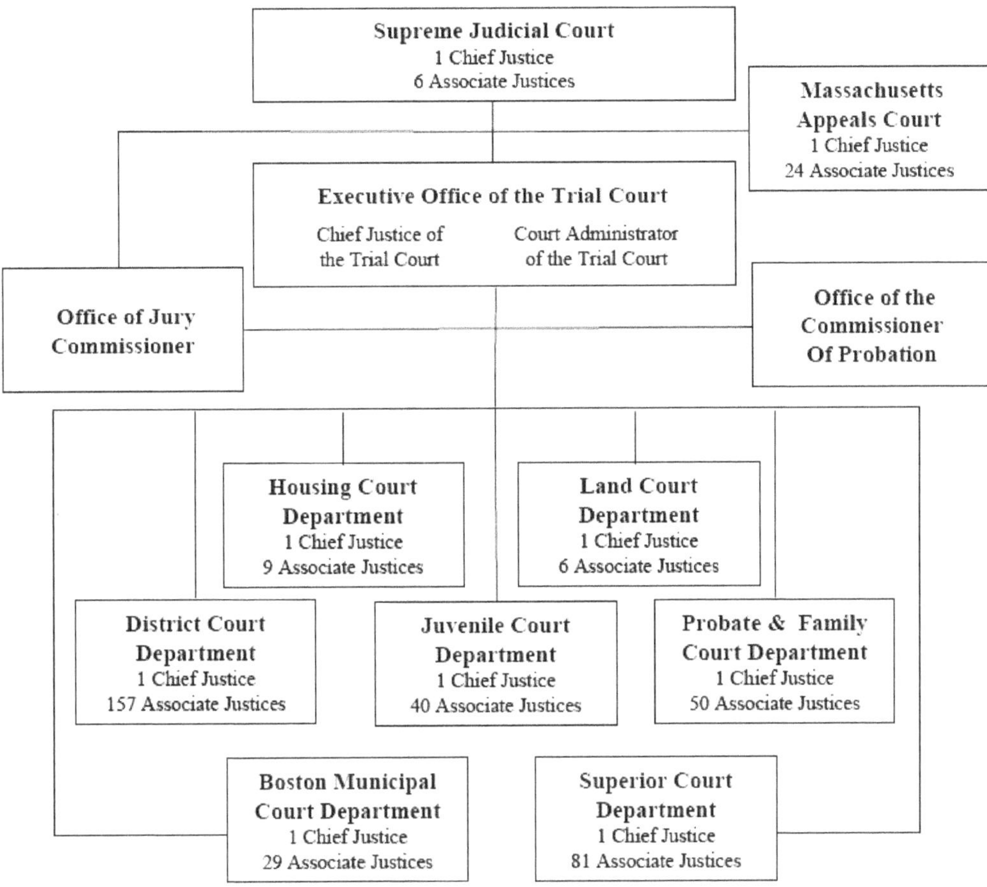

Notes for active learning

The Massachusetts Courts' Structure

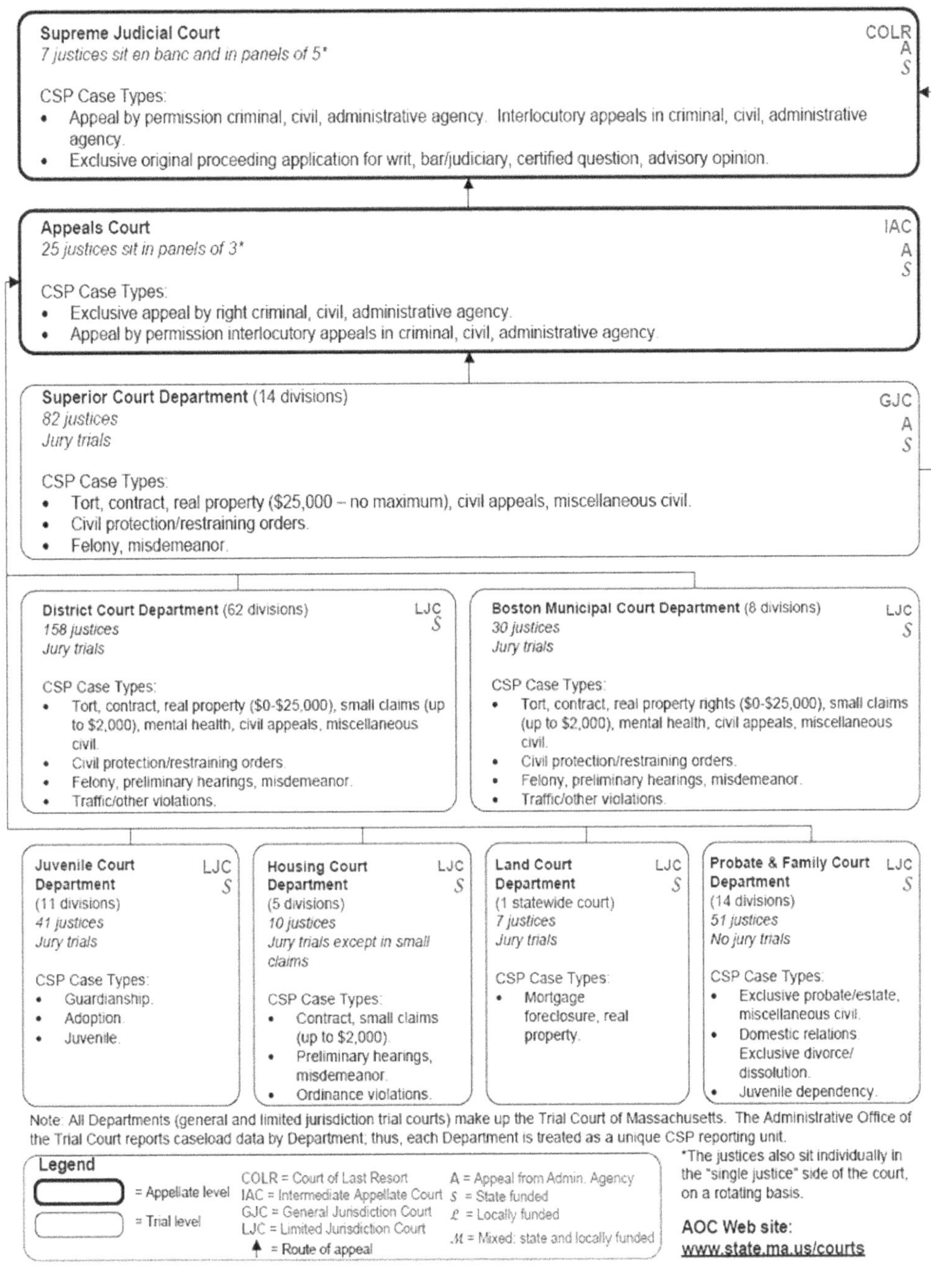

Notes for active learning

The New York Courts' Structure

Civil court structure

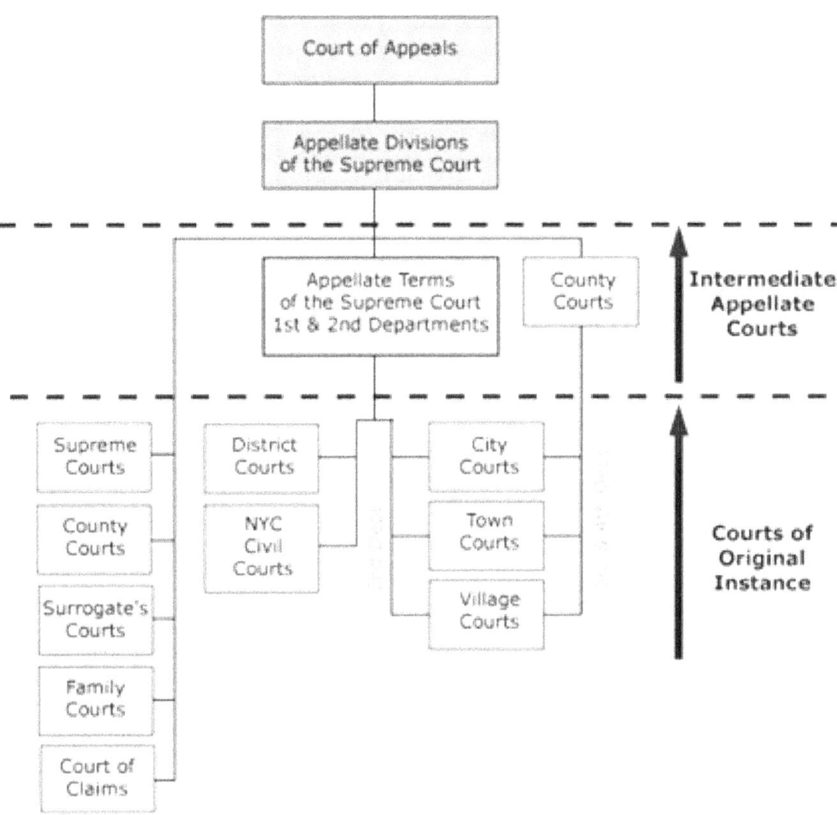

Criminal court structure

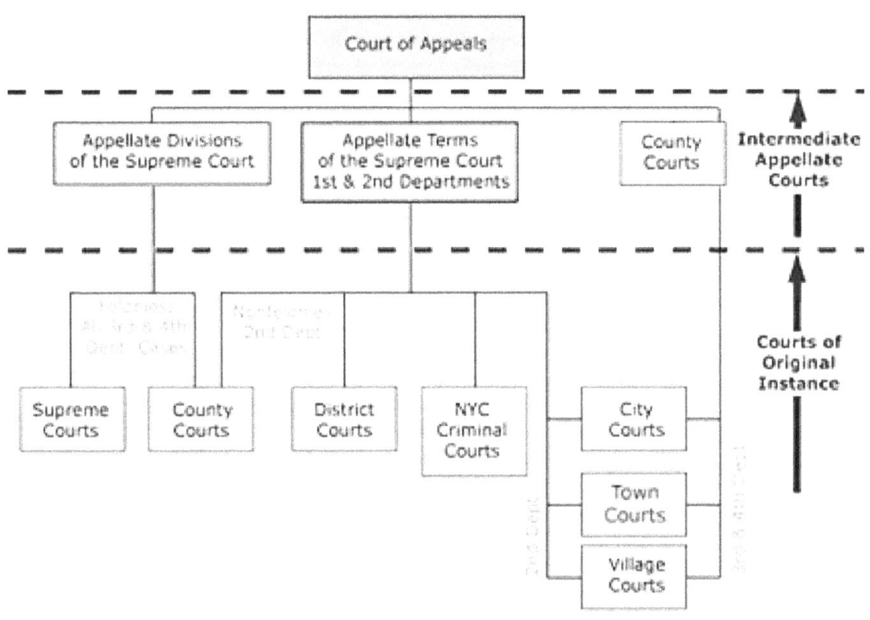

Notes for active learning

The Constitution of the United States (*a transcription*)

THE U.S. NATIONAL ARCHIVES & RECORDS ADMINISTRATION
www.archives.gov

The following text is a transcription of the Constitution as it was inscribed by Jacob Shallus on parchment (the document on display in the Rotunda at the National Archives Museum.) The spelling and punctuation reflect the original.

The Constitution of the United States: A Transcription

The following text is a transcription of the Constitution as it was inscribed by Jacob Shallus on parchment (displayed in the Rotunda at the National Archives Museum.) The authenticated text of the Constitution can be found on the website of the Government Printing Office.

We the People of the United States, in Order to form a more perfect Union, establish Justice, insure domestic Tranquility, provide for the common defence, promote the general Welfare, and secure the Blessings of Liberty to ourselves and our Posterity, do ordain and establish this Constitution for the United States of America.

Article. I

Section. 1.

All legislative Powers herein granted shall be vested in a Congress of the United States, which shall consist of a Senate and House of Representatives.

Section. 2.

The House of Representatives shall be composed of Members chosen every second Year by the People of the several States, and the Electors in each State shall have the Qualifications requisite for Electors of the most numerous Branch of the State Legislature.

No Person shall be a Representative who shall not have attained to the Age of twenty five Years, and been seven Years a Citizen of the United States, and who shall not, when elected, be an Inhabitant of that State in which he shall be chosen.

Representatives and direct Taxes shall be apportioned among the several States which may be included within this Union, according to their respective Numbers, which shall be determined by adding to the whole Number of free Persons, including those bound to Service for a Term of Years, and excluding Indians not taxed, three fifths of all other Persons. The actual Enumeration shall be made within three Years after the first Meeting of the Congress of the United States, and within every subsequent Term of ten Years, in such Manner as they shall by Law direct. The Number of Representatives shall not exceed one for every thirty Thousand, but each State shall have at Least one Representative; and until such enumeration shall be made, the State of New Hampshire shall be entitled to chuse three, Massachusetts eight, Rhode-Island and Providence

Plantations one, Connecticut five, New-York six, New Jersey four, Pennsylvania eight, Delaware one, Maryland six, Virginia ten, North Carolina five, South Carolina five, and Georgia three.

When vacancies happen in the Representation from any State, the Executive Authority thereof shall issue Writs of Election to fill such Vacancies.

The House of Representatives shall chuse their Speaker and other Officers; and shall have the sole Power of Impeachment.

Section. 3.

The Senate of the United States shall be composed of two Senators from each State, chosen by the Legislature thereof, for six Years; and each Senator shall have one Vote.

Immediately after they shall be assembled in Consequence of the first Election, they shall be divided as equally as may be into three Classes. The Seats of the Senators of the first Class shall be vacated at the Expiration of the second Year, of the second Class at the Expiration of the fourth Year, and of the third Class at the Expiration of the sixth Year, so that one third may be chosen every second Year; and if Vacancies happen by Resignation, or otherwise, during the Recess of the Legislature of any State, the Executive thereof may make temporary Appointments until the next Meeting of the Legislature, which shall then fill such Vacancies.

No Person shall be a Senator who shall not have attained to the Age of thirty Years, and been nine Years a Citizen of the United States, and who shall not, when elected, be an Inhabitant of that State for which he shall be chosen.

The Vice President of the United States shall be President of the Senate, but shall have no Vote, unless they be equally divided.

The Senate shall chuse their other Officers, and also a President pro tempore, in the Absence of the Vice President, or when he shall exercise the Office of President of the United States.

The Senate shall have the sole Power to try all Impeachments. When sitting for that Purpose, they shall be on Oath or Affirmation. When the President of the United States is tried, the Chief Justice shall preside: And no Person shall be convicted without the Concurrence of two thirds of the Members present.

Judgment in Cases of Impeachment shall not extend further than to removal from Office, and disqualification to hold and enjoy any Office of honor, Trust or Profit under the United States: but the Party convicted shall nevertheless be liable and subject to Indictment, Trial, Judgment and Punishment, according to Law.

Section. 4.

The Times, Places and Manner of holding Elections for Senators and Representatives, shall be prescribed in each State by the Legislature thereof; but the Congress may at any time by Law make or alter such Regulations, except as to the Places of chusing Senators.

The Congress shall assemble at least once in every Year, and such Meeting shall be on the first Monday in December, unless they shall by Law appoint a different Day.

Section. 5.

Each House shall be the Judge of the Elections, Returns and Qualifications of its own Members, and a Majority of each shall constitute a Quorum to do Business; but a smaller Number may adjourn from day to day, and may be authorized to compel the Attendance of absent Members, in such Manner, and under such Penalties as each House may provide.

Each House may determine the Rules of its Proceedings, punish its Members for disorderly Behaviour, and, with the Concurrence of two thirds, expel a Member.

Each House shall keep a Journal of its Proceedings, and from time to time publish the same, excepting such Parts as may in their Judgment require Secrecy; and the Yeas and Nays of the Members of either House on any question shall, at the Desire of one fifth of those Present, be entered on the Journal.

Neither House, during the Session of Congress, shall, without the Consent of the other, adjourn for more than three days, nor to any other Place than that in which the two Houses shall be sitting.

Section. 6.

The Senators and Representatives shall receive a Compensation for their Services, to be ascertained by Law, and paid out of the Treasury of the United States. They shall in all Cases, except Treason, Felony and Breach of the Peace, be privileged from Arrest during their Attendance at the Session of their respective Houses, and in going to and returning from the same; and for any Speech or Debate in either House, they shall not be questioned in any other Place.

No Senator or Representative shall, during the Time for which he was elected, be appointed to any civil Office under the Authority of the United States, which shall have been created, or the Emoluments whereof shall have been encreased during such time; and no Person holding any Office under the United States, shall be a Member of either House during his Continuance in Office.

Section. 7.

All Bills for raising Revenue shall originate in the House of Representatives; but the Senate may propose or concur with Amendments as on other Bills.

Every Bill which shall have passed the House of Representatives and the Senate, shall, before it become a Law, be presented to the President of the United States; If he approves he shall sign it, but if not he shall return it, with his Objections to that House in which it shall have originated, who shall enter the Objections at large on their Journal, and proceed to reconsider it. If after such Reconsideration two thirds of that House shall agree to pass the Bill, it shall be sent, together with the Objections, to the other House, by which it shall likewise be reconsidered, and if approved by two thirds of that House, it shall become a Law. But in all such Cases the Votes of both Houses shall be determined by yeas and Nays, and the Names of the Persons voting for and against the Bill shall be entered on the Journal of each House respectively. If any Bill shall not be returned by the President within ten Days (Sundays excepted) after it shall have been presented to him, the Same shall be a Law, in like Manner as if he had signed it, unless the Congress by their Adjournment prevent its Return, in which Case it shall not be a Law.

Every Order, Resolution, or Vote to which the Concurrence of the Senate and House of Representatives may be necessary (except on a question of Adjournment) shall be presented to the President of the United States; and before the Same shall take Effect, shall be approved by him, or being disapproved by him, shall be repassed by two thirds of the Senate and House of Representatives, according to the Rules and Limitations prescribed in the Case of a Bill.

Section. 8.

The Congress shall have Power To lay and collect Taxes, Duties, Imposts and Excises, to pay the Debts and provide for the common Defence and general Welfare of the United States; but all Duties, Imposts and Excises shall be uniform throughout the United States;

To borrow Money on the credit of the United States;

To regulate Commerce with foreign Nations, and among the several States, and with the Indian Tribes;

To establish an uniform Rule of Naturalization, and uniform Laws on the subject of Bankruptcies throughout the United States;

To coin Money, regulate the Value thereof, and of foreign Coin, and fix the Standard of Weights and Measures;

To provide for the Punishment of counterfeiting the Securities and current Coin of the United States;

To establish Post Offices and post Roads;

To promote the Progress of Science and useful Arts, by securing for limited Times to Authors and Inventors the exclusive Right to their respective Writings and Discoveries;

To constitute Tribunals inferior to the Supreme Court;

To define and punish Piracies and Felonies committed on the high Seas, and Offences against the Law of Nations;

To declare War, grant Letters of Marque and Reprisal, and make Rules concerning Captures on Land and Water;

To raise and support Armies, but no Appropriation of Money to that Use shall be for a longer Term than two Years;

To provide and maintain a Navy;

To make Rules for the Government and Regulation of the land and naval Forces;

To provide for calling forth the Militia to execute the Laws of the Union, suppress Insurrections and repel Invasions;

To provide for organizing, arming, and disciplining, the Militia, and for governing such Part of them as may be employed in the Service of the United States, reserving to the States respectively, the Appointment of the Officers, and the Authority of training the Militia according to the discipline prescribed by Congress;

To exercise exclusive Legislation in all Cases whatsoever, over such District (not exceeding ten Miles square) as may, by Cession of particular States, and the Acceptance of Congress, become the Seat of the Government of the United States, and to exercise like Authority over all Places purchased by the Consent of the Legislature of the State in which the Same shall be, for the Erection of Forts, Magazines, Arsenals, dock-Yards, and other needful Buildings;—And

To make all Laws which shall be necessary and proper for carrying into Execution the foregoing Powers, and all other Powers vested by this Constitution in the Government of the United States, or in any Department or Officer thereof.

Section. 9.

The Migration or Importation of such Persons as any of the States now existing shall think proper to admit, shall not be prohibited by the Congress prior to the Year one thousand eight hundred and eight, but a Tax or duty may be imposed on such Importation, not exceeding ten dollars for each Person.

The Privilege of the Writ of Habeas Corpus shall not be suspended, unless when in Cases of Rebellion or Invasion the public Safety may require it.

No Bill of Attainder or ex post facto Law shall be passed.

No Capitation, or other direct, Tax shall be laid, unless in Proportion to the Census or enumeration herein before directed to be taken.

No Tax or Duty shall be laid on Articles exported from any State.

No Preference shall be given by any Regulation of Commerce or Revenue to the Ports of one State over those of another: nor shall Vessels bound to, or from, one State, be obliged to enter, clear, or pay Duties in another.

No Money shall be drawn from the Treasury, but in Consequence of Appropriations made by Law; and a regular Statement and Account of the Receipts and Expenditures of all public Money shall be published from time to time.

No Title of Nobility shall be granted by the United States: And no Person holding any Office of Profit or Trust under them, shall, without the Consent of the Congress, accept of any present, Emolument, Office, or Title, of any kind whatever, from any King, Prince, or foreign State.

Section. 10.

No State shall enter into any Treaty, Alliance, or Confederation; grant Letters of Marque and Reprisal; coin Money; emit Bills of Credit; make any Thing but gold and silver Coin a Tender in Payment of Debts; pass any Bill of Attainder, ex post facto Law, or Law impairing the Obligation of Contracts, or grant any Title of Nobility.

No State shall, without the Consent of the Congress, lay any Imposts or Duties on Imports or Exports, except what may be absolutely necessary for executing it's inspection Laws: and the net

Produce of all Duties and Imposts, laid by any State on Imports or Exports, shall be for the Use of the Treasury of the United States; and all such Laws shall be subject to the Revision and Controul of the Congress.

No State shall, without the Consent of Congress, lay any Duty of Tonnage, keep Troops, or Ships of War in time of Peace, enter into any Agreement or Compact with another State, or with a foreign Power, or engage in War, unless actually invaded, or in such imminent Danger as will not admit of delay.

Article. II

Section. 1.

The executive Power shall be vested in a President of the United States of America. He shall hold his Office during the Term of four Years, and, together with the Vice President, chosen for the same Term, be elected, as follows

Each State shall appoint, in such Manner as the Legislature thereof may direct, a Number of Electors, equal to the whole Number of Senators and Representatives to which the State may be entitled in the Congress: but no Senator or Representative, or Person holding an Office of Trust or Profit under the United States, shall be appointed an Elector.

The Electors shall meet in their respective States, and vote by Ballot for two Persons, of whom one at least shall not be an Inhabitant of the same State with themselves. And they shall make a List of all the Persons voted for, and of the Number of Votes for each; which List they shall sign and certify, and transmit sealed to the Seat of the Government of the United States, directed to the President of the Senate. The President of the Senate shall, in the Presence of the Senate and House of Representatives, open all the Certificates, and the Votes shall then be counted. The Person having the greatest Number of Votes shall be the President, if such Number be a Majority of the whole Number of Electors appointed; and if there be more than one who have such Majority, and have an equal Number of Votes, then the House of Representatives shall immediately chuse by Ballot one of them for President; and if no Person have a Majority, then from the five highest on the List the said House shall in like Manner chuse the President. But in chusing the President, the Votes shall be taken by States, the Representation from each State having one Vote; A quorum for this Purpose shall consist of a Member or Members from two thirds of the States, and a Majority of all the States shall be necessary to a Choice. In every Case, after the Choice of the President, the Person having the greatest Number of Votes of the Electors shall be the Vice President. But if there should remain two or more who have equal Votes, the Senate shall chuse from them by Ballot the Vice President.

The Congress may determine the Time of chusing the Electors, and the Day on which they shall give their Votes; which Day shall be the same throughout the United States.

No Person except a natural born Citizen, or a Citizen of the United States, at the time of the Adoption of this Constitution, shall be eligible to the Office of President; neither shall any Person be eligible to that Office who shall not have attained to the Age of thirty five Years, and been fourteen Years a Resident within the United States.

In Case of the Removal of the President from Office, or of his Death, Resignation, or Inability to discharge the Powers and Duties of the said Office, the Same shall devolve on the Vice President, and the Congress may by Law provide for the Case of Removal, Death, Resignation or Inability, both of the President and Vice President, declaring what Officer shall then act as President, and such Officer shall act accordingly, until the Disability be removed, or a President shall be elected.

The President shall, at stated Times, receive for his Services, a Compensation, which shall neither be encreased nor diminished during the Period for which he shall have been elected, and he shall not receive within that Period any other Emolument from the United States, or any of them.

Before he enters on the Execution of his Office, he shall take the following Oath or Affirmation:—"I do solemnly swear (or affirm) that I will faithfully execute the Office of President of the United States, and will to the best of my Ability, preserve, protect and defend the Constitution of the United States."

Section. 2.

The President shall be Commander in Chief of the Army and Navy of the United States, and of the Militia of the several States, when called into the actual Service of the United States; he may require the Opinion, in writing, of the principal Officer in each of the executive Departments, upon any Subject relating to the Duties of their respective Offices, and he shall have Power to grant Reprieves and Pardons for Offences against the United States, except in Cases of Impeachment.

He shall have Power, by and with the Advice and Consent of the Senate, to make Treaties, provided two thirds of the Senators present concur; and he shall nominate, and by and with the Advice and Consent of the Senate, shall appoint Ambassadors, other public Ministers and Consuls, Judges of the supreme Court, and all other Officers of the United States, whose Appointments are not herein otherwise provided for, and which shall be established by Law: but the Congress may by Law vest the Appointment of such inferior Officers, as they think proper, in the President alone, in the Courts of Law, or in the Heads of Departments.

The President shall have Power to fill up all Vacancies that may happen during the Recess of the Senate, by granting Commissions which shall expire at the End of their next Session.

Section. 3.

He shall from time to time give to the Congress Information of the State of the Union, and recommend to their Consideration such Measures as he shall judge necessary and expedient; he may, on extraordinary Occasions, convene both Houses, or either of them, and in Case of Disagreement between them, with Respect to the Time of Adjournment, he may adjourn them to such Time as he shall think proper; he shall receive Ambassadors and other public Ministers; he shall take Care that the Laws be faithfully executed, and shall Commission all the Officers of the United States.

Section. 4.

The President, Vice President and all civil Officers of the United States, shall be removed from Office on Impeachment for, and Conviction of, Treason, Bribery, or other high Crimes and Misdemeanors.

Article III

Section. 1.

The judicial Power of the United States, shall be vested in one supreme Court, and in such inferior Courts as the Congress may from time to time ordain and establish. The Judges, both of the supreme and inferior Courts, shall hold their Offices during good Behaviour, and shall, at stated Times, receive for their Services, a Compensation, which shall not be diminished during their Continuance in Office.

Section. 2.

The judicial Power shall extend to all Cases, in Law and Equity, arising under this Constitution, the Laws of the United States, and Treaties made, or which shall be made, under their Authority;—to all Cases affecting Ambassadors, other public Ministers and Consuls;—to all Cases of admiralty and maritime Jurisdiction;—to Controversies to which the United States shall be a Party;—to Controversies between two or more States;—between a State and Citizens of another State,—between Citizens of different States,—between Citizens of the same State claiming Lands under Grants of different States, and between a State, or the Citizens thereof, and foreign States, Citizens or Subjects.

In all Cases affecting Ambassadors, other public Ministers and Consuls, and those in which a State shall be Party, the supreme Court shall have original Jurisdiction. In all the other Cases before mentioned, the supreme Court shall have appellate Jurisdiction, both as to Law and Fact, with such Exceptions, and under such Regulations as the Congress shall make.

The Trial of all Crimes, except in Cases of Impeachment, shall be by Jury; and such Trial shall be held in the State where the said Crimes shall have been committed; but when not committed within any State, the Trial shall be at such Place or Places as the Congress may by Law have directed.

Section. 3.

Treason against the United States, shall consist only in levying War against them, or in adhering to their Enemies, giving them Aid and Comfort. No Person shall be convicted of Treason unless on the Testimony of two Witnesses to the same overt Act, or on Confession in open Court.

The Congress shall have Power to declare the Punishment of Treason, but no Attainder of Treason shall work Corruption of Blood, or Forfeiture except during the Life of the Person attainted.

Article. IV

Section. 1.

Full Faith and Credit shall be given in each State to the public Acts, Records, and judicial Proceedings of every other State. And the Congress may by general Laws prescribe the Manner in which such Acts, Records and Proceedings shall be proved, and the Effect thereof.

Section. 2.

The Citizens of each State shall be entitled to all Privileges and Immunities of Citizens in the several States.

A Person charged in any State with Treason, Felony, or other Crime, who shall flee from Justice, and be found in another State, shall on Demand of the executive Authority of the State from which he fled, be delivered up, to be removed to the State having Jurisdiction of the Crime.

No Person held to Service or Labour in one State, under the Laws thereof, escaping into another, shall, in Consequence of any Law or Regulation therein, be discharged from such Service or Labour, but shall be delivered up on Claim of the Party to whom such Service or Labour may be due.

Section. 3.

New States may be admitted by the Congress into this Union; but no new State shall be formed or erected within the Jurisdiction of any other State; nor any State be formed by the Junction of two or more States, or Parts of States, without the Consent of the Legislatures of the States concerned as well as of the Congress.

The Congress shall have Power to dispose of and make all needful Rules and Regulations respecting the Territory or other Property belonging to the United States; and nothing in this Constitution shall be so construed as to Prejudice any Claims of the United States, or of any particular State.

Section. 4.

The United States shall guarantee to every State in this Union a Republican Form of Government, and shall protect each of them against Invasion; and on Application of the Legislature, or of the Executive (when the Legislature cannot be convened), against domestic Violence.

Article. V

The Congress, whenever two thirds of both Houses shall deem it necessary, shall propose Amendments to this Constitution, or, on the Application of the Legislatures of two thirds of the several States, shall call a Convention for proposing Amendments, which, in either Case, shall be valid to all Intents and Purposes, as Part of this Constitution, when ratified by the Legislatures of three fourths of the several States, or by Conventions in three fourths thereof, as the one or the other Mode of Ratification may be proposed by the Congress; Provided that no Amendment which may be made prior to the Year One thousand eight hundred and eight shall in any Manner affect the first and fourth Clauses in the Ninth Section of the first Article; and that no State, without its Consent, shall be deprived of its equal Suffrage in the Senate.

Article. VI

All Debts contracted and Engagements entered into, before the Adoption of this Constitution, shall be as valid against the United States under this Constitution, as under the Confederation.

This Constitution, and the Laws of the United States which shall be made in Pursuance thereof; and all Treaties made, or which shall be made, under the Authority of the United States, shall be the supreme Law of the Land; and the Judges in every State shall be bound thereby, any Thing in the Constitution or Laws of any State to the Contrary notwithstanding.

The Senators and Representatives before mentioned, and the Members of the several State Legislatures, and all executive and judicial Officers, both of the United States and of the several States, shall be bound by Oath or Affirmation, to support this Constitution; but no religious Test shall ever be required as a Qualification to any Office or public Trust under the United States.

Article. VII

The Ratification of the Conventions of nine States, shall be sufficient for the Establishment of this Constitution between the States so ratifying the Same.

The Word, "the," being interlined between the seventh and eighth Lines of the first Page, The Word "Thirty" being partly written on an Erazure in the fifteenth Line of the first Page, The Words "is tried" being interlined between the thirty second and thirty third Lines of the first Page and the Word "the" being interlined between the forty third and forty fourth Lines of the second Page.

Attest William Jackson Secretary, done in Convention by the Unanimous Consent of the States present the Seventeenth Day of September in the Year of our Lord one thousand seven hundred and Eighty seven and of the Independance of the United States of America the Twelfth In witness whereof We have hereunto subscribed our Names, G°. Washington, *Presidt and deputy from Virginia*

Delaware
Geo: Read
Gunning Bedford jun
John Dickinson
Richard Bassett
Jaco: Broom

Maryland
James McHenry
Dan of St Thos.
Jenifer
Danl. Carroll

Virginia
John Blair
James Madison Jr.

North Carolina
Wm. Blount
Richd. Dobbs
Spaight
Hu Williamson

South Carolina
J. Rutledge
Charles Cotesworth
Pinckney
Charles Pinckney
Pierce Butler

Georgia
William Few
Abr Baldwin

New Hampshire
John Langdon
Nicholas Gilman

Massachusetts
Nathaniel Gorham
Rufus King

Connecticut
Wm. Saml. Johnson
Roger Sherman

New York
Alexander Hamilton

New Jersey
Wil: Livingston
David Brearley
Wm. Paterson
Jona: Dayton

Pensylvania
B Franklin
Thomas Mifflin
Robt. Morris
Geo. Clymer
Thos. FitzSimons
Jared Ingersoll
James Wilson
Gouv Morris

Enactment of the Bill of Rights of the United States of America (1791)

The first ten Amendments to the Constitution make up the Bill of Rights. Written by James Madison in response to calls from several states for greater constitutional protection for individual liberties, the Bill of Rights lists specific prohibitions on governmental power. The Virginia Declaration of Rights, written by George Mason, strongly influenced Madison.

One of the contention points between Federalists and Anti-Federalists was the Constitution's lack of a bill of rights that would place specific limits on government power.

Federalists argued that the Constitution did not need a bill of rights because the people and the states kept powers not explicitly given to the federal government.

Anti-Federalists held that a *bill of rights* was necessary to safeguard individual liberty.

Madison, then a member of the U.S. House of Representatives, went through the Constitution itself, making changes where he thought most appropriate.

Several Representatives, led by Roger Sherman, objected that Congress had no authority to change the wording of the Constitution. Therefore, Madison's changes were presented as a list of amendments that would follow Article VII.

The House approved 17 amendments. Of these 17, the Senate approved 12. Those 12 were sent to the states for approval in August of 1789. Of those 12 proposed amendments, 10 were quickly ratified. Virginia's legislature became the last to ratify the Amendments on December 15, 1791. These Amendments are the Bill of Rights.

The Bill of Rights is a list of limits on government power. For example, what the Founders saw as the natural right of individuals to speak and worship freely was protected by the First Amendment's prohibitions on Congress from making laws establishing a religion or abridging freedom of speech.

Another example is the natural right to be free from the government's unreasonable intrusion in one's home was safeguarded by the Fourth Amendment's warrant requirements.

Other precursors to the Bill of Rights include English documents such as the Magna Carta[1], the Petition of Rights, the English Bill of Rights, and the Massachusetts Body of Liberties.

The Magna Carta illustrates Compact Theory[1] as well as initial strides toward limited government. Its provisions address individual rights and political rights. Latin for "Great Charter," the Magna Carta was written by Barons in Runnymede, England, and forced on the King.

Although the protections were generally limited to the prerogatives of the Barons, the Magna Carta embodied the general principle that the King accepted limitations on his rule. These included the fundamental acknowledgment that the king was not above the law.

Included in the Magna Carta are protections for the English church, petitioning the king, freedom from the forced quarter of troops and unreasonable searches, due process and fair trial protections, and freedom from excessive fines. These protections can be found in the First, Third, Fourth, Fifth, Sixth, and Eighth Amendments to the Constitution.

The Magna Carta is the oldest compact in England. The Mayflower Compact, the Fundamental Orders of Connecticut, and the Albany Plan are examples from the American colonies.

The Articles of Confederation was a compact among the states, and the Constitution creates a compact based on a federal system between the national government, state governments, and the people. The Hayne-Webster Debate focused on the compact created by the Constitution.

[1] Philosophers including Thomas Hobbes, John Locke, and Jean-Jacques Rousseau theorized that peoples' condition in a "state of nature" (that is, outside of society) is one of freedom, but that freedom inevitably degrades into war, chaos, or debilitating competition without the benefit of a system of laws and government. They reasoned, therefore, that for their happiness, individuals willingly trade some of their natural freedom in exchange for the protections provided by the government.

The Bill of Rights: Amendments I–X

Amendment I

Congress shall make no law respecting an establishment of religion, or prohibiting the free exercise thereof; or abridging the freedom of speech, or of the press; or the right of the people peaceably to assemble, and to petition the government for a redress of grievances.

Amendment II

A well regulated militia, being necessary to the security of a free state, the right of the people to keep and bear arms, shall not be infringed.

Amendment III

No soldier shall, in time of peace be quartered in any house, without the consent of the owner, nor in time of war, but in a manner to be prescribed by law.

Amendment IV

The right of the people to be secure in their persons, houses, papers, and effects, against unreasonable searches and seizures, shall not be violated, and no warrants shall issue, but upon probable cause, supported by oath or affirmation, and particularly describing the place to be searched, and the persons or things to be seized.

Amendment V

No person shall be held to answer for a capital, or otherwise infamous crime, unless on a presentment or indictment of a grand jury, except in cases arising in the land or naval forces, or in the militia, when in actual service in time of war or public danger; nor shall any person be subject for the same offense to be twice put in jeopardy of life or limb; nor shall be compelled in any criminal case to be a witness against himself, nor be deprived of life, liberty, or property, without due process of law; nor shall private property be taken for public use, without just compensation.

Amendment VI

In all criminal prosecutions, the accused shall enjoy the right to a speedy and public trial, by an impartial jury of the state and district wherein the crime shall have been committed, which district shall have been previously ascertained by law, and to be informed of the nature and cause of the accusation; to be confronted with the witnesses against him; to have compulsory process for obtaining witnesses in his favor, and to have the assistance of counsel for his defense.

Amendment VII

In suits at common law, where the value in controversy shall exceed twenty dollars, the right of trial by jury shall be preserved, and no fact tried by a jury, shall be otherwise reexamined in any court of the United States, than according to the rules of the common law.

Amendment VIII

Excessive bail shall not be required, nor excessive fines imposed, nor cruel and unusual punishments inflicted.

Amendment IX

The enumeration in the Constitution, of certain rights, shall not be construed to deny or disparage others retained by the people.

Amendment X

The powers not delegated to the United States by the Constitution, nor prohibited by it to the states, are reserved to the states respectively, or to the people.

Constitutional Amendments XI–XXVII

AMENDMENT XI

Passed by Congress March 4, 1794. Ratified February 7, 1795.

Note: Article III, section 2, of the Constitution was modified by amendment 11.

The Judicial power of the United States shall not be construed to extend to any suit in law or equity, commenced or prosecuted against one of the United States by Citizens of another State, or by Citizens or Subjects of any Foreign State.

AMENDMENT XII

Passed by Congress December 9, 1803. Ratified June 15, 1804.

Note: A portion of Article II, section 1 of the Constitution was superseded by the 12th amendment.

The Electors shall meet in their respective states and vote by ballot for President and Vice-President, one of whom, at least, shall not be an inhabitant of the same state with themselves; they shall name in their ballots the person voted for as President, and in distinct ballots the person voted for as Vice-President, and they shall make distinct lists of all persons voted for as President, and of all persons voted for as Vice-President, and of the number of votes for each, which lists they shall sign and certify, and transmit sealed to the seat of the government of the United States, directed to the President of the Senate; -- the President of the Senate shall, in the presence of the Senate and House of Representatives, open all the certificates and the votes shall then be counted; -- The person having the greatest number of votes for President, shall be the President, if such number be a majority of the whole number of Electors appointed; and if no person have such majority, then from the persons having the highest numbers not exceeding three on the list of those voted for as President, the House of Representatives shall choose immediately, by ballot, the President. But in choosing the President, the votes shall be taken by states, the representation from each state having one vote; a quorum for this purpose shall consist of a member or members from two-thirds of the states, and a majority of all the states shall be necessary to a choice. [And if the House of Representatives shall not choose a President whenever the right of choice shall devolve upon them, before the fourth day of March next following, then the Vice-President shall act as President, as in case of the death or other constitutional disability of the President. --]* The person having the greatest number of votes as Vice-President, shall be the Vice-President, if such number be a majority of the whole number of Electors appointed, and if no person have a majority, then from the two highest numbers on the list, the Senate shall choose the Vice-President; a quorum for the purpose shall consist of two-thirds of the whole number of Senators, and a majority of the whole number shall be necessary to a choice. But no person constitutionally ineligible to the office of President shall be eligible to that of Vice-President of the United States.

**Superseded by section 3 of the 20th Amendment.*

AMENDMENT XIII

Passed by Congress January 31, 1865. Ratified December 6, 1865.

Note: A portion of Article IV, section 2, of the Constitution was superseded by the 13th amendment.

Section 1.

Neither slavery nor involuntary servitude, except as a punishment for crime whereof the party shall have been duly convicted, shall exist within the United States, or any place subject to their jurisdiction.

Section 2.

Congress shall have power to enforce this article by appropriate legislation.

AMENDMENT XIV

Passed by Congress June 13, 1866. Ratified July 9, 1868.

Note: Article I, section 2, of the Constitution was modified by section 2 of the 14th amendment.

Section 1.

All persons born or naturalized in the United States, and subject to the jurisdiction thereof, are citizens of the United States and of the State wherein they reside. No State shall make or enforce any law which shall abridge the privileges or immunities of citizens of the United States; nor shall any State deprive any person of life, liberty, or property, without due process of law; nor deny to any person within its jurisdiction the equal protection of the laws.

Section 2.

Representatives shall be apportioned among the several States according to their respective numbers, counting the whole number of persons in each State, excluding Indians not taxed. But when the right to vote at any election for the choice of electors for President and Vice-President of the United States, Representatives in Congress, the Executive and Judicial officers of a State, or the members of the Legislature thereof, is denied to any of the male inhabitants of such State, being twenty-one years of age,* and citizens of the United States, or in any way abridged, except for participation in rebellion, or other crime, the basis of representation therein shall be reduced in the proportion which the number of such male citizens shall bear to the whole number of male citizens twenty-one years of age in such State.

Section 3.

No person shall be a Senator or Representative in Congress, or elector of President and Vice-President, or hold any office, civil or military, under the United States, or under any State, who, having previously taken an oath, as a member of Congress, or as an officer of the United States, or as a member of any State legislature, or as an executive or judicial officer of any State, to support the Constitution of the United States, shall have engaged in insurrection or rebellion against the same, or given aid or comfort to the enemies thereof. But Congress may by a vote of two-thirds of each House, remove such disability.

Section 4.

The validity of the public debt of the United States, authorized by law, including debts incurred for payment of pensions and bounties for services in suppressing insurrection or rebellion, shall not be questioned. But neither the United States nor any State shall assume or pay any debt or obligation incurred in aid of insurrection or rebellion against the United States, or any claim for the loss or emancipation of any slave; but all such debts, obligations and claims shall be held illegal and void.

Section 5.

The Congress shall have the power to enforce, by appropriate legislation, the provisions of this article.

**Changed by section 1 of the 26th Amendment.*

AMENDMENT XV

Passed by Congress February 26, 1869. Ratified February 3, 1870.

Section 1.

The right of citizens of the United States to vote shall not be denied or abridged by the United States or by any State on account of race, color, or previous condition of servitude.

Section 2.

The Congress shall have the power to enforce this article by appropriate legislation.

AMENDMENT XVI

Passed by Congress July 2, 1909. Ratified February 3, 1913.

Note: Article I, section 9, of the Constitution was modified by amendment 16.

The Congress shall have power to lay and collect taxes on incomes, from whatever source derived, without apportionment among the several States, and without regard to any census or enumeration.

AMENDMENT XVII

Passed by Congress May 13, 1912. Ratified April 8, 1913.

Note: Article I, section 3, of the Constitution was modified by the 17th Amendment.

The Senate of the United States shall be composed of two Senators from each State, elected by the people thereof, for six years; and each Senator shall have one vote. The electors in each State shall have the qualifications requisite for electors of the most numerous branch of the State legislatures.

When vacancies happen in the representation of any State in the Senate, the executive authority of such State shall issue writs of election to fill such vacancies: *Provided*, That the legislature of any State may empower the executive thereof to make temporary appointments until the people fill the vacancies by election as the legislature may direct.

This amendment shall not be so construed as to affect the election or term of any Senator chosen before it becomes valid as part of the Constitution.

AMENDMENT XVIII

Passed by Congress December 18, 1917. Ratified January 16, 1919. Repealed by Amendment 21.

Section 1.

After one year from the ratification of this article the manufacture, sale, or transportation of intoxicating liquors within, the importation thereof into, or the exportation thereof from the United States and all territory subject to the jurisdiction thereof for beverage purposes is hereby prohibited.

Section 2.

The Congress and the several States shall have concurrent power to enforce this article by appropriate legislation.

Section 3.

This article shall be inoperative unless it shall have been ratified as an amendment to the Constitution by the legislatures of the several States, as provided in the Constitution, within seven years from the date of the submission hereof to the States by the Congress.

AMENDMENT XIX

Passed by Congress June 4, 1919. Ratified August 18, 1920.

The right of citizens of the United States to vote shall not be denied or abridged by the United States or by any State on account of sex.

Congress shall have power to enforce this article by appropriate legislation.

AMENDMENT XX

Passed by Congress March 2, 1932. Ratified January 23, 1933.

Note: Article I, section 4, of the Constitution was modified by section 2 of this Amendment. In addition, a portion of the 12th Amendment was superseded by section 3.

Section 1.

The terms of the President and the Vice President shall end at noon on the 20th day of January, and the terms of Senators and Representatives at noon on the 3d day of January, of the years in which such terms would have ended if this article had not been ratified; and the terms of their successors shall then begin.

Section 2.

The Congress shall assemble at least once in every year, and such meeting shall begin at noon on the 3d day of January, unless they shall by law appoint a different day.

Section 3.

If, at the time fixed for the beginning of the term of the President, the President elect shall have died, the Vice President elect shall become President. If a President shall not have been chosen before the time fixed for the beginning of his term, or if the President elect shall have failed to qualify, then the Vice President elect shall act as President until a President shall have qualified; and the Congress may by law provide for the case wherein neither a President elect nor a Vice President elect shall have qualified, declaring who shall then act as President, or the manner in which one who is to act shall be selected, and such person shall act accordingly until a President or Vice President shall have qualified.

Section 4.

The Congress may by law provide for the case of the death of any of the persons from whom the House of Representatives may choose a President whenever the right of choice shall have devolved upon them, and for the case of the death of any of the persons from whom the Senate may choose a Vice President whenever the right of choice shall have devolved upon them.

Section 5.

Sections 1 and 2 shall take effect on the 15th day of October following the ratification of this article.

Section 6.

This article shall be inoperative unless it shall have been ratified as an amendment to the Constitution by the legislatures of three-fourths of the several States within seven years from the date of its submission.

AMENDMENT XXI

Passed by Congress February 20, 1933. Ratified December 5, 1933.

Section 1.

The eighteenth article of amendment to the Constitution of the United States is hereby repealed.

Section 2.

The transportation or importation into any State, Territory, or possession of the United States for delivery or use therein of intoxicating liquors, in violation of the laws thereof, is hereby prohibited.

Section 3.

This article shall be inoperative unless it shall have been ratified as an amendment to the Constitution by conventions in the several States, as provided in the Constitution, within seven years from the date of the submission hereof to the States by the Congress.

AMENDMENT XXII

Passed by Congress March 21, 1947. Ratified February 27, 1951.

Section 1.

No person shall be elected to the office of the President more than twice, and no person who has held the office of President, or acted as President, for more than two years of a term to which some other person was elected President shall be elected to the office of the President more than once. But this Article shall not apply to any person holding the office of President when this Article was proposed by the Congress, and shall not prevent any person who may be holding the office of President, or acting as President, during the term within which this Article becomes operative from holding the office of President or acting as President during the remainder of such term.

Section 2.

This article shall be inoperative unless it shall have been ratified as an amendment to the Constitution by the legislatures of three-fourths of the several States within seven years from the date of its submission to the States by the Congress.

AMENDMENT XXIII

Passed by Congress June 16, 1960. Ratified March 29, 1961.

Section 1.

The District constituting the seat of Government of the United States shall appoint in such manner as the Congress may direct:

A number of electors of President and Vice President equal to the whole number of Senators and Representatives in Congress to which the District would be entitled if it were a State, but in no event more than the least populous State; they shall be in addition to those appointed by the States, but they shall be considered, for the purposes of the election of President and Vice President, to be electors appointed by a State; and they shall meet in the District and perform such duties as provided by the twelfth article of amendment.

Section 2.

The Congress shall have power to enforce this article by appropriate legislation.

AMENDMENT XXIV

Passed by Congress August 27, 1962. Ratified January 23, 1964.

Section 1.

The right of citizens of the United States to vote in any primary or other election for President or Vice President, for electors for President or Vice President, or for Senator or Representative in Congress, shall not be denied or abridged by the United States or any State by reason of failure to pay any poll tax or other tax.

Section 2.

The Congress shall have power to enforce this article by appropriate legislation.

AMENDMENT XXV

Passed by Congress July 6, 1965. Ratified February 10, 1967.

Note: Article II, section 1, of the Constitution was affected by the 25th amendment.

Section 1.

In case of the removal of the President from office or of his death or resignation, the Vice President shall become President.

Section 2.

Whenever there is a vacancy in the office of the Vice President, the President shall nominate a Vice President who shall take office upon confirmation by a majority vote of both Houses of Congress.

Section 3.

Whenever the President transmits to the President pro tempore of the Senate and the Speaker of the House of Representatives his written declaration that he is unable to discharge the powers and duties of his office, and until he transmits to them a written declaration to the contrary, such powers and duties shall be discharged by the Vice President as Acting President.

Section 4.

Whenever the Vice President and a majority of either the principal officers of the executive departments or of such other body as Congress may by law provide, transmit to the President pro tempore of the Senate and the Speaker of the House of Representatives their written declaration that the President is unable to discharge the powers and duties of his office, the Vice President shall immediately assume the powers and duties of the office as Acting President.

Thereafter, when the President transmits to the President pro tempore of the Senate and the Speaker of the House of Representatives his written declaration that no inability exists, he shall resume the powers and duties of his office unless the Vice President and a majority of either the principal officers of the executive department or of such other body as Congress may by law provide, transmit within four days to the President pro tempore of the Senate and the Speaker of the House of Representatives their written declaration that the President is unable to discharge the powers and duties of his office. Thereupon Congress shall decide the issue, assembling within forty-eight hours for that purpose if not in session. If the Congress, within twenty-one days after receipt of the latter written declaration, or, if Congress is not in session, within twenty-one days after Congress is required to assemble, determines by two-thirds vote of both Houses that the President is unable to discharge the powers and duties of his office, the Vice President shall continue to discharge the same as Acting President; otherwise, the President shall resume the powers and duties of his office.

AMENDMENT XXVI

Passed by Congress March 23, 1971. Ratified July 1, 1971.

Note: Amendment 14, section 2, of the Constitution was modified by section 1 of the 26th amendment.

Section 1.
The right of citizens of the United States, who are eighteen years of age or older, to vote shall not be denied or abridged by the United States or by any State on account of age.

Section 2.
The Congress shall have power to enforce this article by appropriate legislation.

AMENDMENT XXVII

Originally proposed Sept. 25, 1789. Ratified May 7, 1992.

No law, varying the compensation for the services of the Senators and Representatives, shall take effect, until an election of Representatives shall have intervened

States' Rights Under the U.S. Constitution

Selective incorporation under the 14th Amendment

The U.S. Constitution has Articles and Amendments that established constitutional rights.

The provisions in the Bill of Rights (i.e., the first ten Amendments to the Constitution) were initially binding upon only the federal government.

In time, most of these provisions became binding upon the states through *selective incorporation* into the *due process clause* of the 14th Amendment (i.e., reverse incorporation).

When a provision is made binding on a state, a state can no longer restrict the rights guaranteed in that provision.

The 1st Amendment guarantees the freedoms of speech, press, religion, and assembly.

The 5th Amendment protects the right to grand jury proceedings in federal criminal cases.

The 6th Amendment guarantees a right to confront witnesses (i.e., Confrontation Clause).

The right to confront witnesses was not *selectively incorporated* into the due process clause of the 14th Amendment and is not binding upon the states.

Therefore, persons involved in state criminal proceedings as a defendant have no federal constitutional right to grand jury proceedings.

Whether an individual has a right to a grand jury becomes a question of state law.

The 10th Amendment, which is part of the **Bill of Rights**, was ratified on December 15, 1791. It states the Constitution's principle of **federalism** by providing that powers not granted to the **federal government** by the Constitution, nor prohibited to the **States**, are reserved to the States or the people.

Federalism in the United States

Federalism in the United States is the evolving relationship between **state governments** and the **federal government**.

The American government has evolved from a system of dual federalism to associative federalism.

In "Federalist No. 46," James Madison wrote that the states and national government "are in fact but different agents and trustees of the people, constituted with different powers."

Alexander Hamilton, in "Federalist No. 28," suggested that both levels of government would exercise authority to the citizens' benefit: "If their [the peoples'] rights are invaded by either, they can make use of the other as the instrument of redress."[3]

Because the states were preexisting political entities, the U.S. Constitution did not need to define or explain federalism in one section, but it often mentions the rights and responsibilities of state governments and state officials in relation to the federal government.

The federal government has certain *express powers* (also called **enumerated powers**), which are powers spelled out in the Constitution, including the right to levy taxes, declare war, and regulate interstate and foreign commerce.

Also, the *Necessary and Proper Clause* gives the federal government the *implied power* to pass any law "necessary and proper" to execute its express powers.

Enumerated powers of the Federal Government are contained in Article I, Section 8 of the U.S. Constitution.

Other powers—the *reserved powers*—are reserved to the people or the states under the 10th Amendment. The Supreme Court decision significantly expanded the power delegated to the federal government in *McCulloch v. Maryland* (1819) and the 13th, 14th and 15th, Amendments to the Constitution following the Civil War.

Interpretation of the Constitution

Mode of Constitutional interpretation

There is disagreement over the analytical construct for interpreting the Constitution.

Living Constitution (closely aligned with Realism and Realist judges) changes to meet the needs of society.

Mode 1: *legislative history* considers the intent during the enactment.

Mode 2: *interpreting the text* has increased enormously as a mode of analysis.

> Scalia: what I look for in the Constitution is what I look for in a statute: the *original meaning of the text*, not what the original draftsmen intended.

Ideological groupings

Ideology is a system of fundamental beliefs that specify appropriate and inappropriate conduct.

Judicial decisions often derive or, at least, align with the political ideology of judges, as has been empirically shown.

Conservatives on the court espouse a limited role for government in the private affairs of citizens, let markets rule.

Liberals on the court espouse an expanded role for the government in the private affairs of citizens.

Legal criticisms

Natural law is the unwritten body of universal moral principles underlying the ethical and legal norms by which human conduct is evaluated and governed.

Textualism is where judges have no authority to pursue broader social purposes or write new laws.

Strict constructionism was described by the late Justice Scalia as a degraded form of textualism.

Legislative intent looks for objectified intent as a reasonable person would gather from the text of the law placed alongside the remainder of the corpus juris;

> the primary object of interpreting statutes is to ascertain the legislative intent *or* the meaning which the subject is authorized to understand the legislature intended; it is undemocratic to have the meaning of a law determined by what the lawgiver means rather than what the lawgiver promulgated. The intent of the lawgiver, not the judges.

Originalism (or *original intent*): what was meant by the drafters at the time it was written. Original meaning proposes what a reasonable person living when the language was ratified would believe the meaning.

Legal realism permits modification if furthering the function intended.

Living constitutionalism proposes that the Constitution must change.

Critical legal studies focus on race, gender, sex, weight, Marxism, and conflict.

The 4th and 5th Amendments Protections for Criminal Defendants

The Fourth Amendment to the U.S. Constitution protects persons and corporations from overzealous investigative activities by the government. It protects the rights of the people from unreasonable search and seizure by the government and permits people to be secure in their persons, houses, papers, and effects.

Reasonable searches are those (in most instances) predicated on a search warrant based on probable cause. Search warrants specifically state the *place and scope* of the authorized search. General searches beyond the specified area are forbidden.

Warrantless searches generally are permitted only 1) incident to arrest, 2) where evidence is in "plain view," or 3) where evidence likely will be destroyed. Evidence obtained from an unreasonable search and seizure is considered tainted and, under the exclusionary rule, is generally excluded from criminal prosecutions.

The Fifth Amendment provides that no person "shall be compelled in any criminal case to be a witness against himself." A person cannot be compelled to give testimony against himself or herself, although nontestimonial evidence, such as fingerprints and body fluids, may be required. This protection applies only to natural persons, not corporations and partnerships.

Based on Supreme Court decisions, it is improper for a jury to infer guilt from the defendant's exercise of their constitutional right to remain silent.

However, if the government wants to obtain evidence from one who has taken the Fifth, it can offer the person immunity, which means the government would agree not to prosecute the person based on the testimony they would give. The Fifth Amendment protects against double jeopardy, whereby a criminal defendant may not be tried twice for the same crime.

If the same criminal act involves several crimes, the accused may be tried for each crime without violating the double jeopardy clause. If the same act violates the laws of other jurisdictions, each jurisdiction may charge and try the accused.

Comprehensive Glossary of Legal Terms

Over 2,100 essential legal terms defined and explained. An excellent reference source for law students, practitioners, and readers seeking an understanding of legal vocabulary and its application.

Landmark U.S. Supreme Court Cases: Essential Summaries

Learn important constitutional cases that shaped American law. Understand how the evolving needs of society intersect with the U.S. Constitution. Summaries of seminal Supreme Court cases focused on legal issues, underlying principles, and judicial decisions.

Visit our Amazon store

      Copyright © 2022 Sterling Education.